DESIGN and SIGN

– PEGGY COBB –

ISBN: 978-1-7163-9588-8 (sc)
ISBN: 978-1-7163-9587-1 (e)

Lulu Publishing Services rev. date: 11/27/2020

CONTENTS

FOREWORD

Peggy Cobb learned to use a computer in her nineties, and it has become her lifeline to the outside world – especially as age-related hearing loss makes chatting via regular telephone impractical. She seasons many of our email conversations with aphorisms, such as "be flexible, and you won't get bent out of shape" and "humor: never leave home without it." Her favorite is one passed on by her father: "furnish your mind well, and you will always have a comfortable place to live."

When the COVID-19 restrictions went into effect, I was struggling with the isolation, and I was concerned about how Peggy would handle being alone at her age. I should have known better. She reported that her daily schedule was nearly full, as she was hard at work on her many projects, including this book, and enjoying every minute of it.

For the past four years, I have been supporting Peggy as she brings this book into existence. It reflects her interests in art – especially in the designs of everyday objects – and her experiences as a mother of a child with multiple disabilities. Her goal was to create a sort of "anti-coloring book" that enables users of all ages and abilities to create original designs for fun or practical application and, if desired, to think more critically about spatial relationships and the aesthetic choices made by artisans from various parts of the world.

During one visit with Peggy in 2017, I had barely walked into the lobby of her apartment building when she leapt out of her chair, rushed over to hug me, and pulled a copy of the previous day's *Atlanta Journal-Constitution* out of her bag. She pointed to an article about the High Museum of Art's current African art exhibit and exclaimed that if I would drive us there, she would navigate.

The exhibition was presented along the rectangular perimeter of a huge open room, and informative placards lined the walls. We read and discussed each one. Out of habit or perceived necessity, I suppose, both of us still tend to talk really loudly to each other. At one point, I remember thinking that the museum was otherwise eerily quiet and that, surely, we were not the only ones there. I recall turning my head back toward the doorway from which we had entered and seeing a security guard with a large group of visitors, who, as I would later find out, had been standing there for quite some time, engrossed in Peggy's observations.

After examining every artifact on display, Peggy was ready to "get to work." We went to the museum's coffee shop, where she got us a table and dumped out the contents of her bag. "Supplies!" she declared. True enough. Pens, pencils, markers, plenty of paper – the works. Freshly inspired by the exhibit, she demonstrated how "Design and Sign" works while commenting on the lines, shapes, colors, textures, and patterns evident throughout the exhibit. I was fascinated by her ability to observe, absorb, and apply what she had seen and learned in such a short period of time. But, more importantly, I was captivated by her desire to teach others how to replicate everyday designs and create new ones.

At the age of 101, Peggy redoubled her efforts to complete Design and Sign, and throughout this process, I have come to rely on her emails as a source of continuous joy and much-needed perspective. Over the course of 2020, her commitment to the project never wavered. By finishing it in these difficult times, she demonstrated the value of her favorite aphorism – "furnish your mind well, and you will always have a comfortable place to live" – and fulfilled her desire to share her lifelong love of art with YOU.

-- A longtime friend*

* The writer is not named due to employer restrictions.

WHAT IS DESIGN AND SIGN?

This book is about an art activity that is "as old as the hills" yet as new as today. By today, I mean it is for a new audience – YOU, where you become the artist! It's an endlessly imaginative activity for kids, family, and friends.

I have always liked creativity, especially art – creating it, sharing it and encouraging others to do so. For decades, I brought art projects for the kids who attended the annual reunions at my family home in Lynd, Minnesota (the adults would jump in, too!). One project used what I now call "building blocks" – small marks that are repeated several times over a page – as a starting point for creating unique images. This book brings together the simple process we used while sitting together at tables in small groups making all-over designs from building blocks, and signing and sharing our creations. This process has been used for years in countless "field tests" involving family, friends and schools, including teachers pursuing advanced degrees.

Building blocks (or something like them) are the foundation of many of the all-over designs that we see every day, on wallpaper, fabric, bedspreads, upholstery, rugs, draperies, tiling, wrapping paper, architecture, furniture, nature and more. We often take these designs for granted and barely notice their constituent parts – that is, the small patterns of lines and shapes that are repeated over and over again. This art activity **heightens our awareness of the visual world around us**.

This art activity is for everyone. With the simple guidance provided by this book, any person, young or old, even many people with disabilities, can create art. It can be done anywhere! After creating your unique design, SIGN your work and date it, a one-of-a-kind piece of art.

-- Peggy Cobb

INSTRUCTIONS

SUPPLIES NEEDED:

You need colored markers, pens or pencils (crayons don't work quite as well, but are OK if that's all you have), and the sheets of building blocks starting at page 24 of this book. Blank sheets of paper are helpful, too, for doodling and practicing different lines and shapes before starting your design; see Step 2, below.

DIRECTIONS:

1. Select a building block sheet.

2. Start at the topmost building block (top left, if there are two at the top), and put some kind of line or shape* or dots through, along or near that building block.

   * A "line" can be straight, curved, angled, zigzagged, a curlique or irregular, or a combination of those.

   A "shape" is simply a line or series of connected lines in which the beginning and ending points join to form an enclosed space, a shape.

   There are examples on the cover of this book, and in the examples of designs made from building blocks starting at page 7.

3. Repeat the same line or shape on each building block on the sheet.

   IMPORTANT: Be sure to be consistent. Repeat each line or shape exactly, and in exactly the same place on or near each building block.

4. Go back to the top, add a different line or shape, and then add that same line or shape to each building block on the sheet.

5.   Stop and look. Your own design is beginning to emerge.

6.   Repeat steps 4 and 5 until you, the artist, are satisfied with the all-over design.

Experiment by adding connecting lines or shapes between the building blocks. Just be consistent as noted in Step 3, above.

In the next section, you will see a few building block pages along with a few examples of the very different designs that can be created from the same building block page. You'll see that the end result can be pictorial (that is, it can look like a picture of something familiar), or it can be completely abstract.

After that, there are several pages of these same building block sheets and others for you to use to create your own designs. You should make as many copies of the building block sheets as you wish.

EXAMPLES OF THE VARIETY OF DESIGNS THAT CAN BE CREATED FROM THE SAME BUILDING BLOCKS

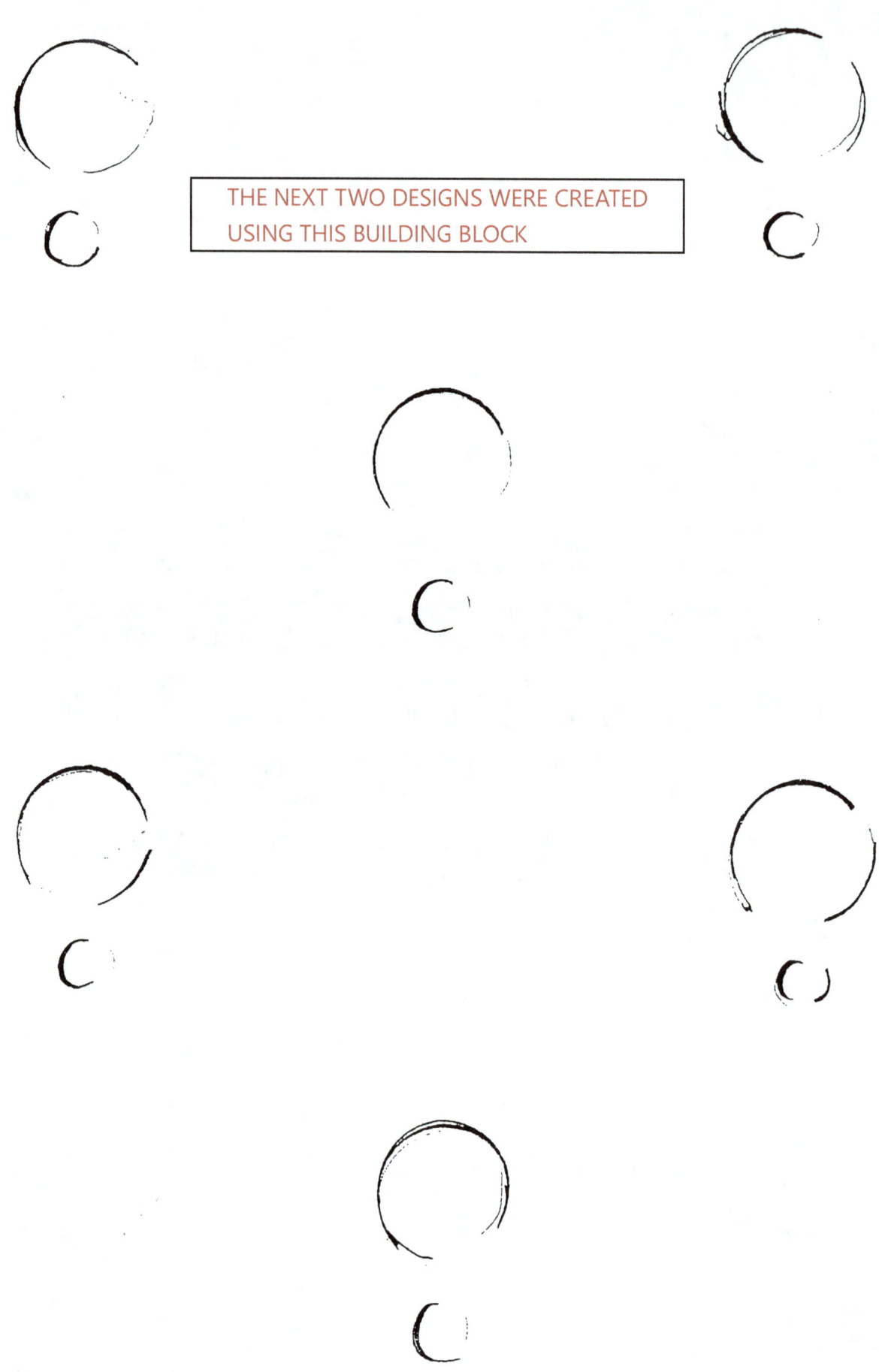

THE NEXT TWO DESIGNS WERE CREATED
USING THIS BUILDING BLOCK

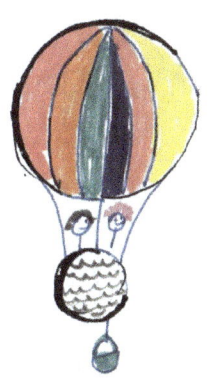
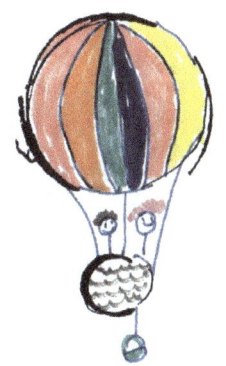
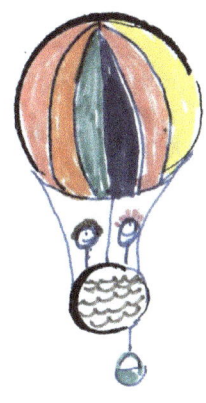
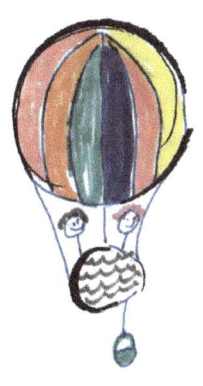
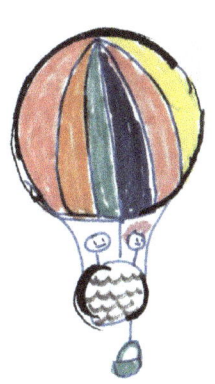
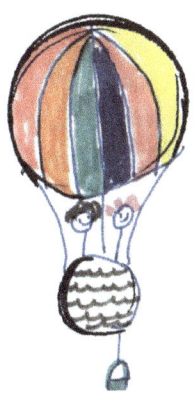

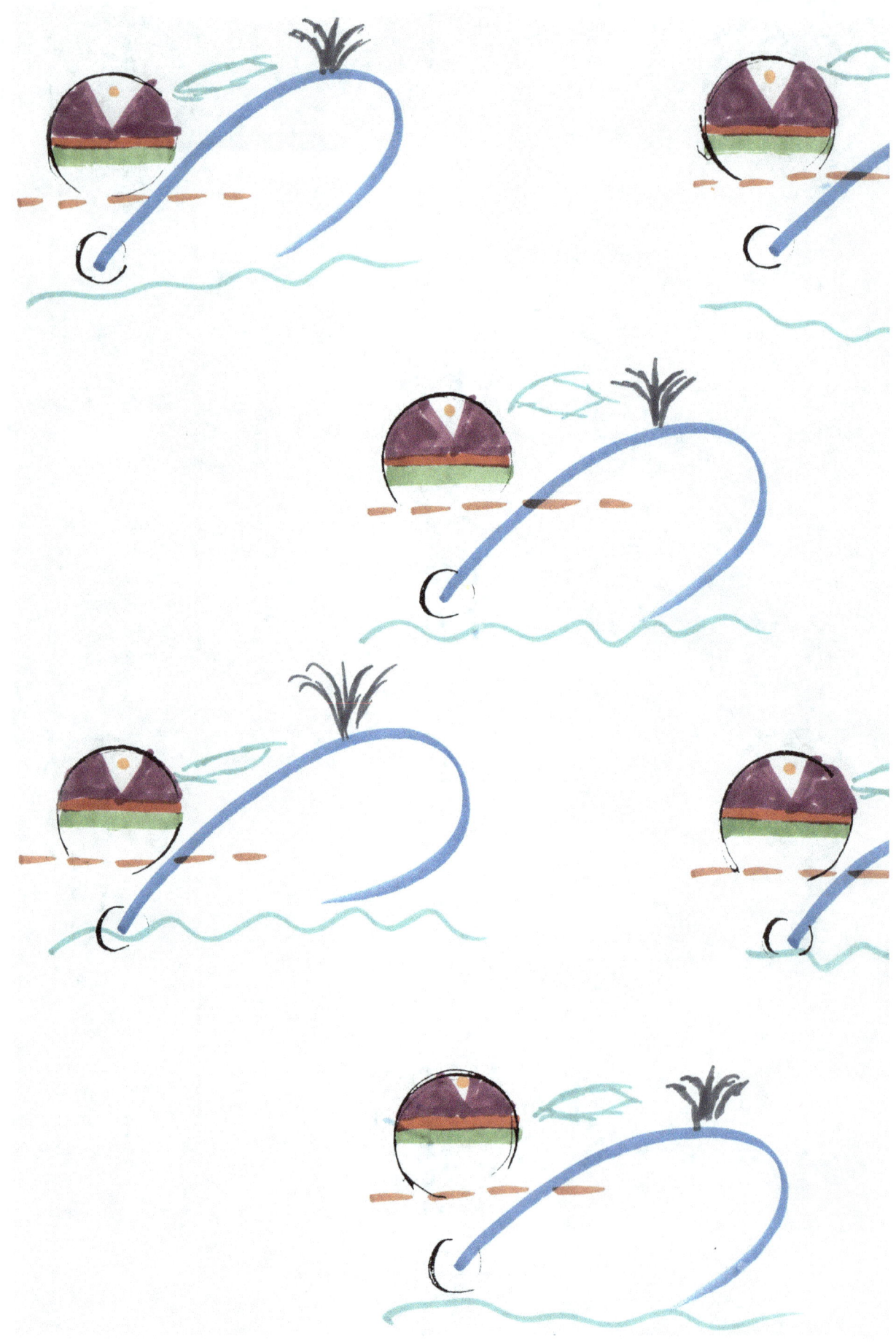

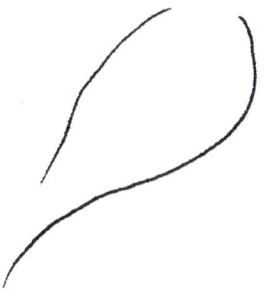

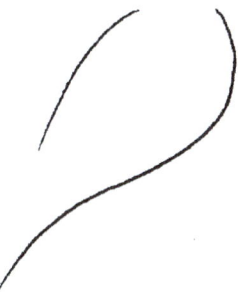

THE NEXT THREE DESIGNS WERE CREATED
USING THIS BUILDING BLOCK

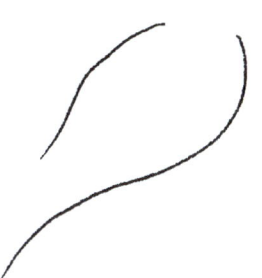

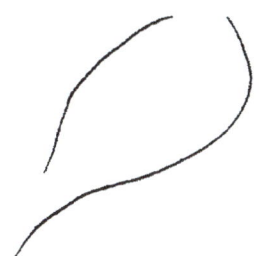

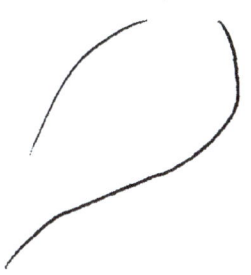

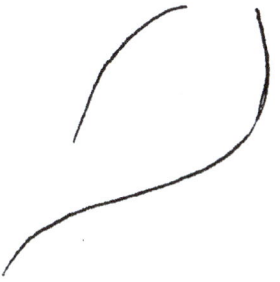

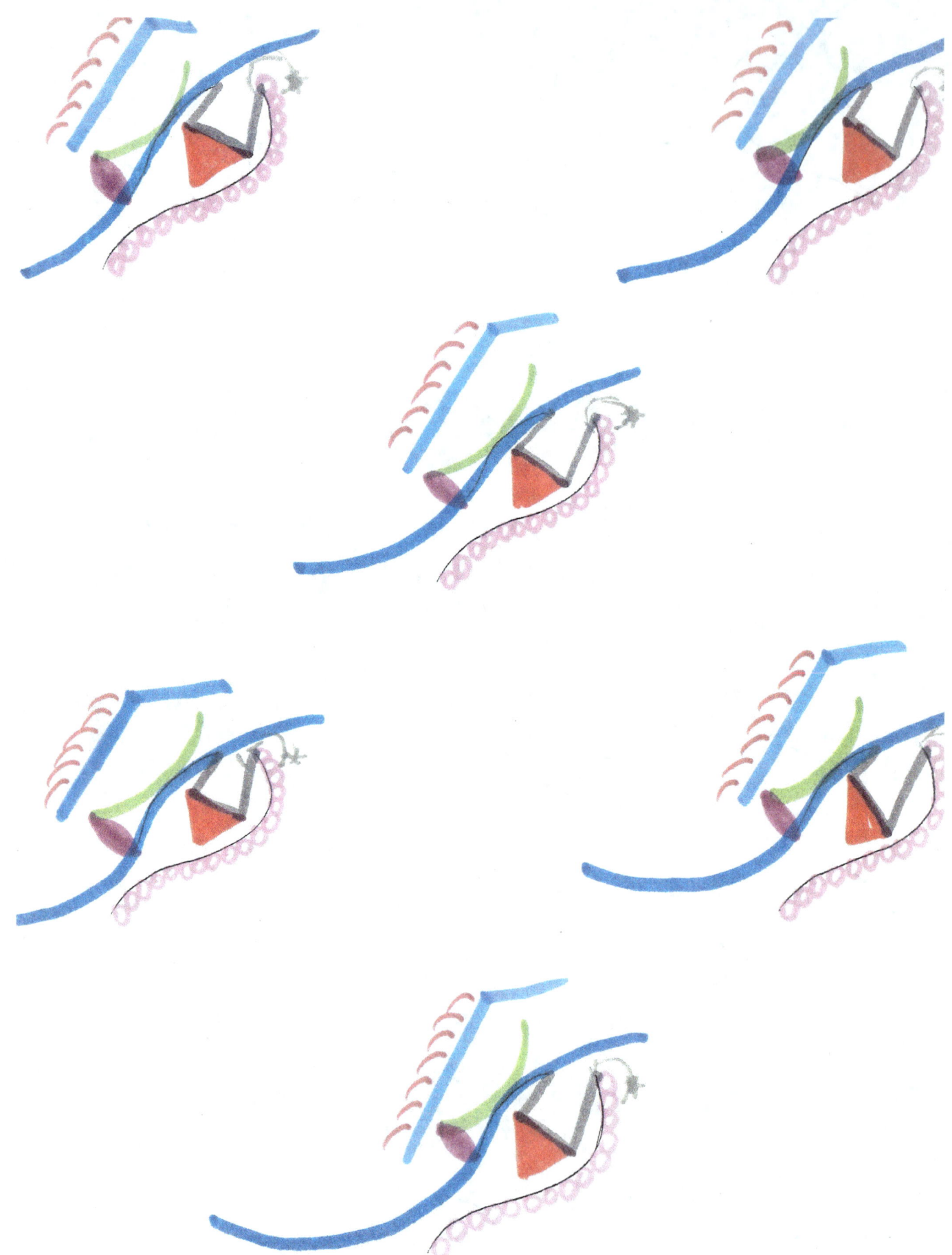

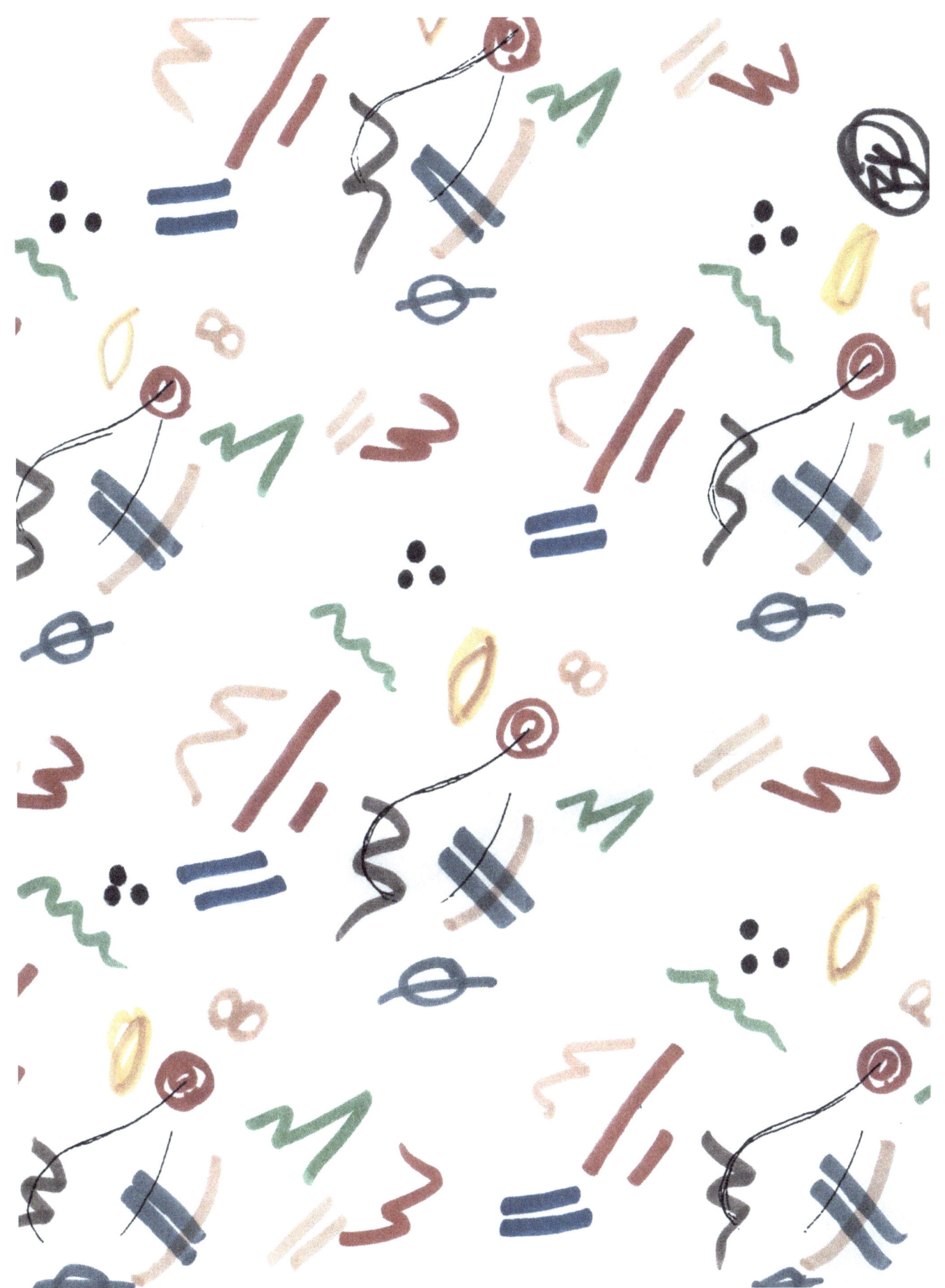

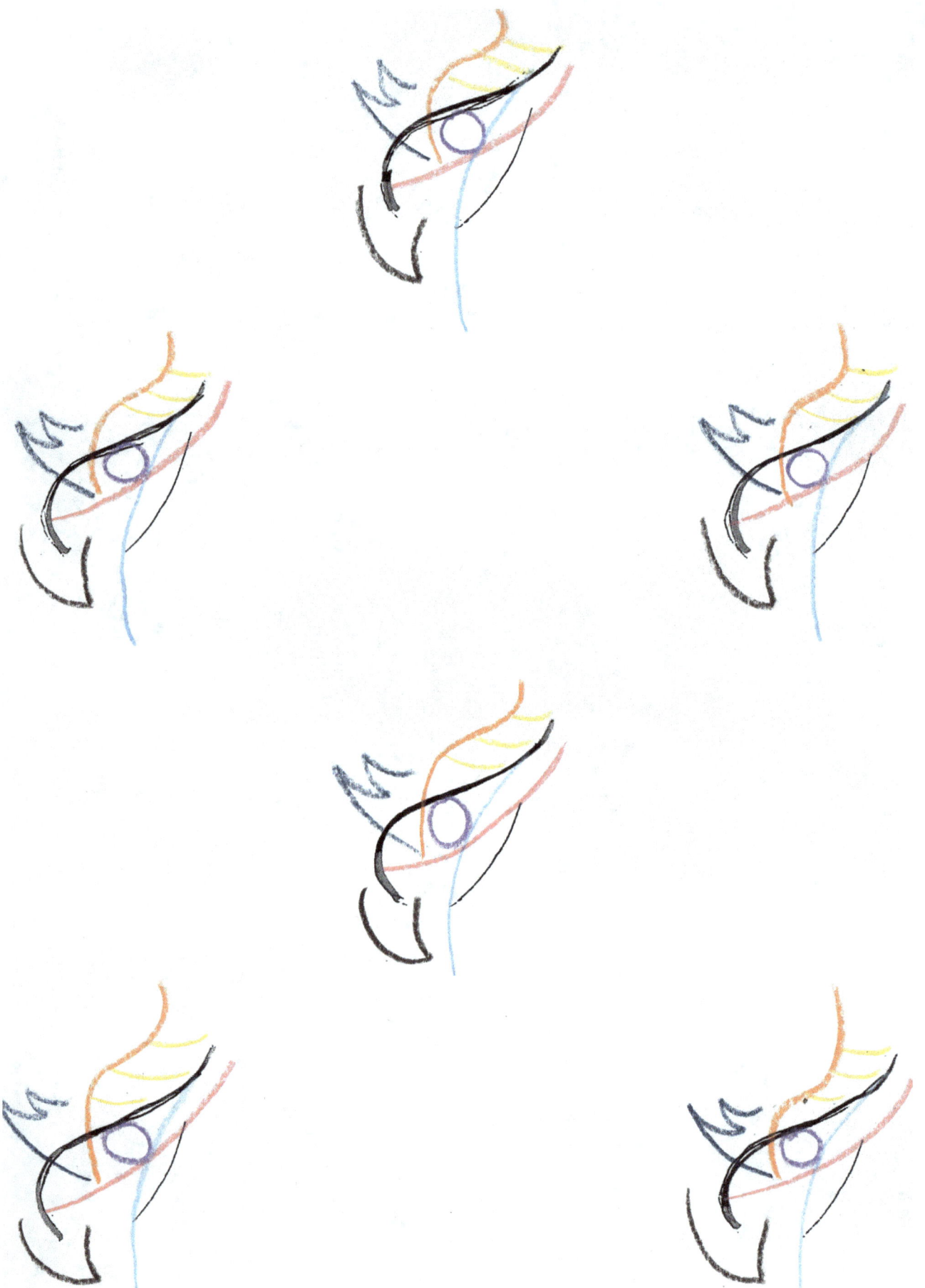

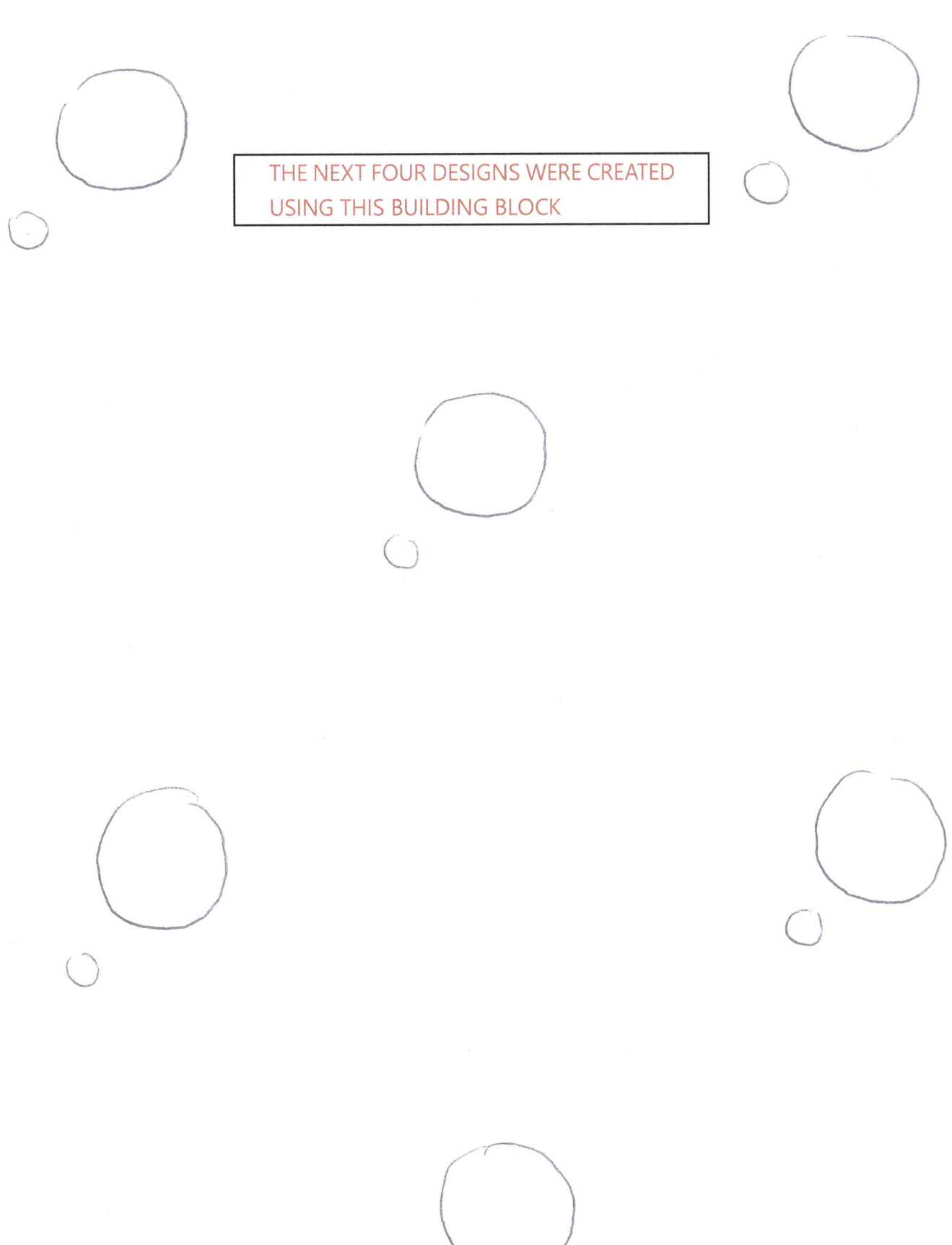

THE NEXT FOUR DESIGNS WERE CREATED
USING THIS BUILDING BLOCK

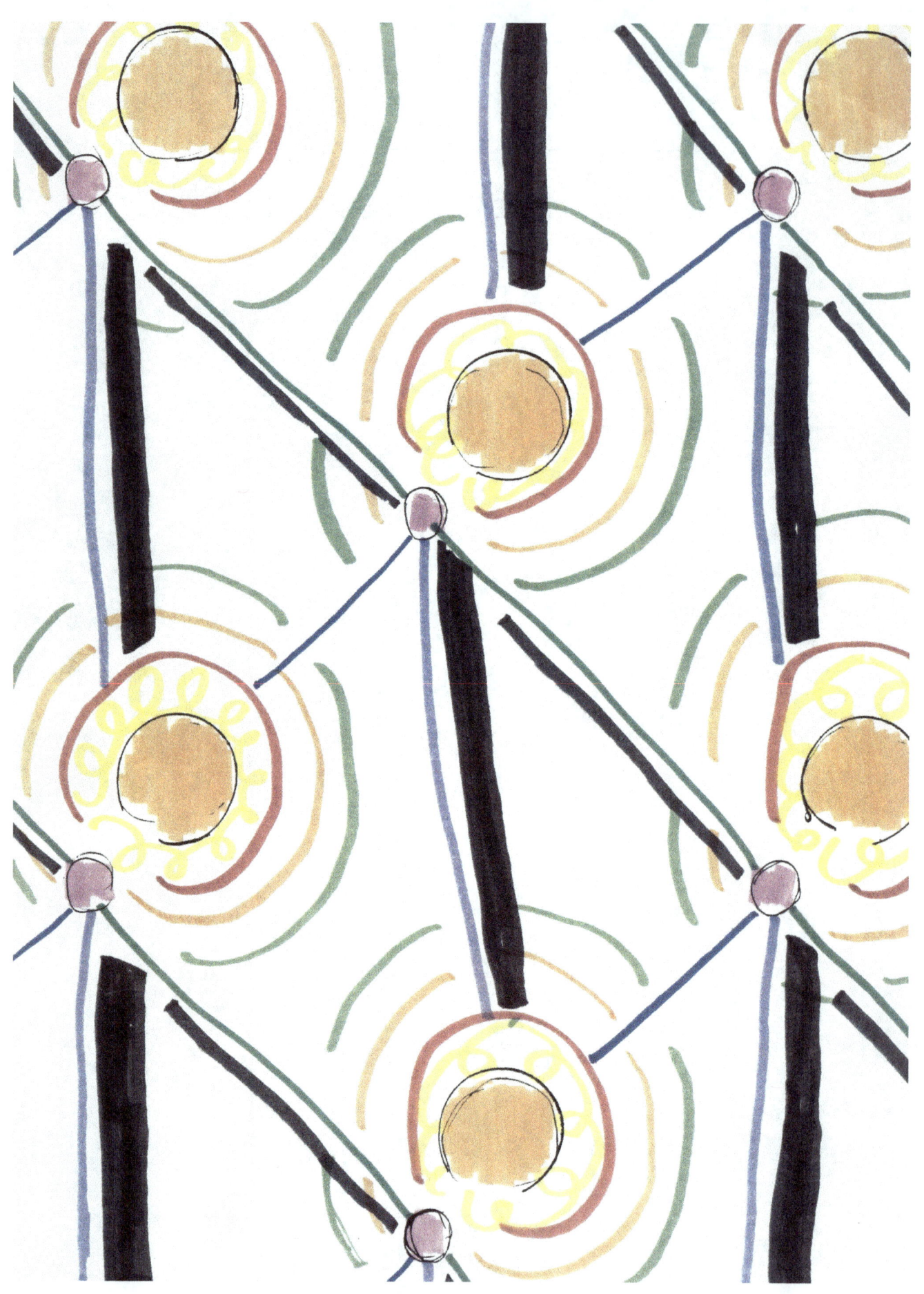

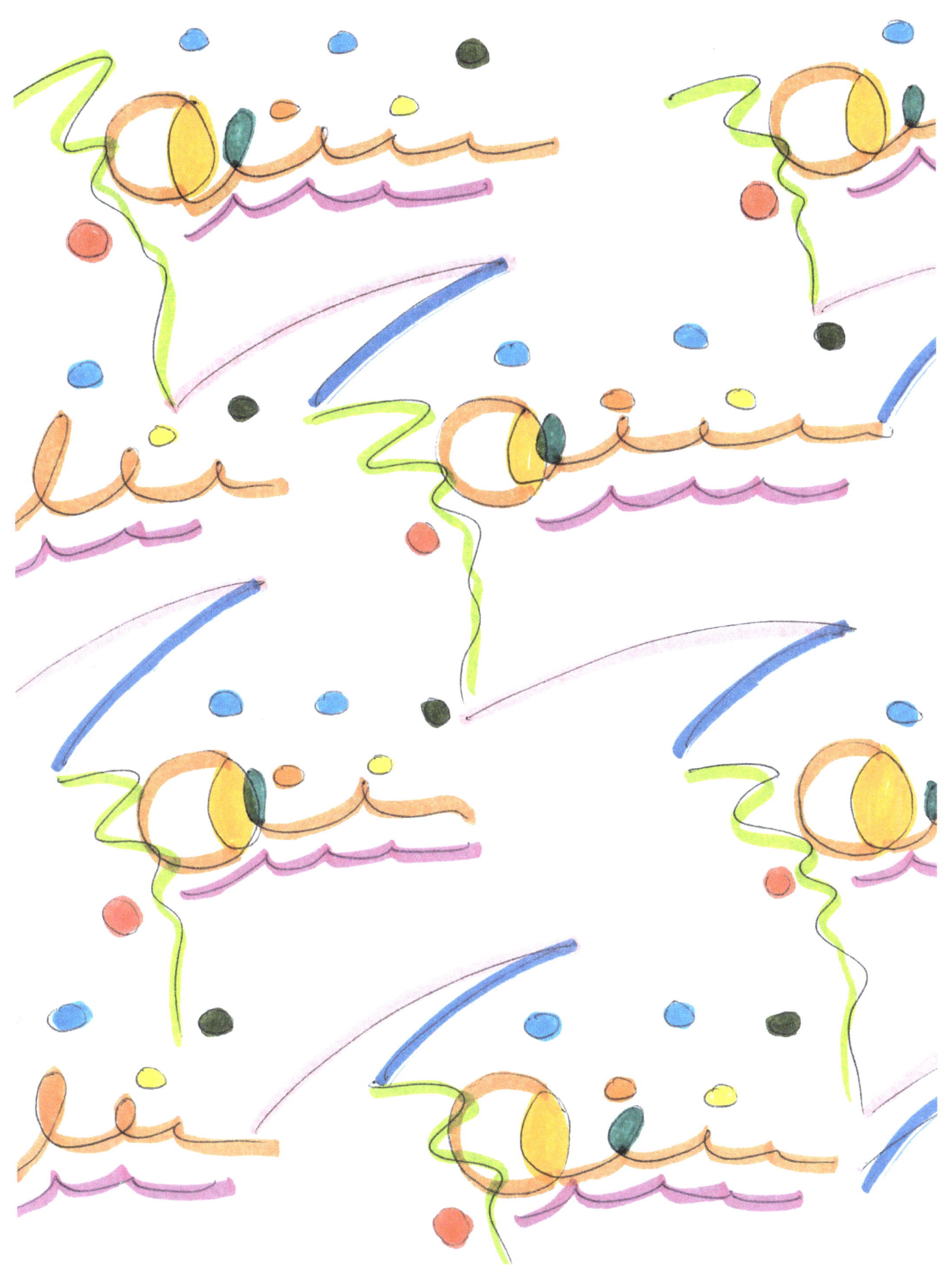

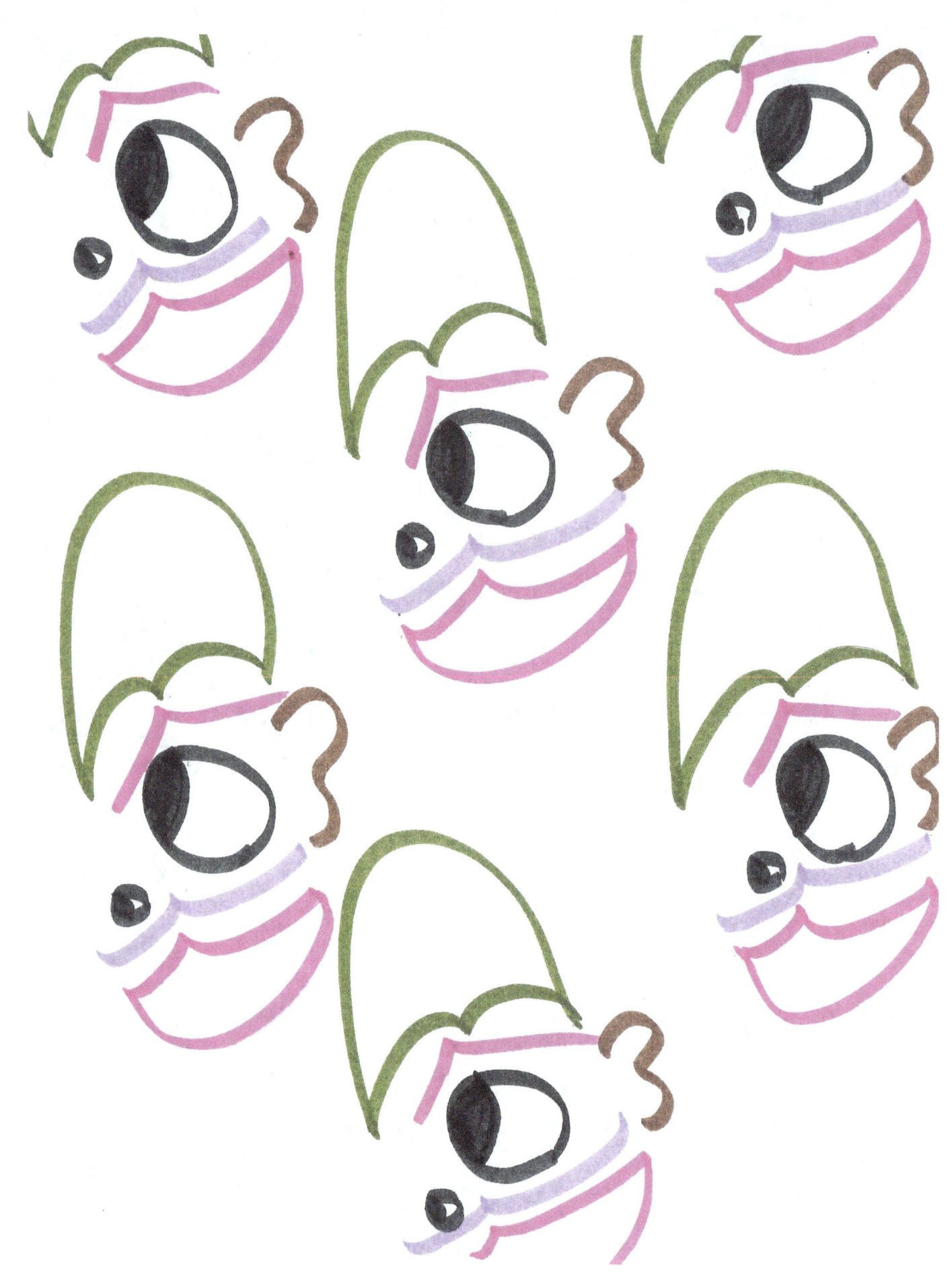

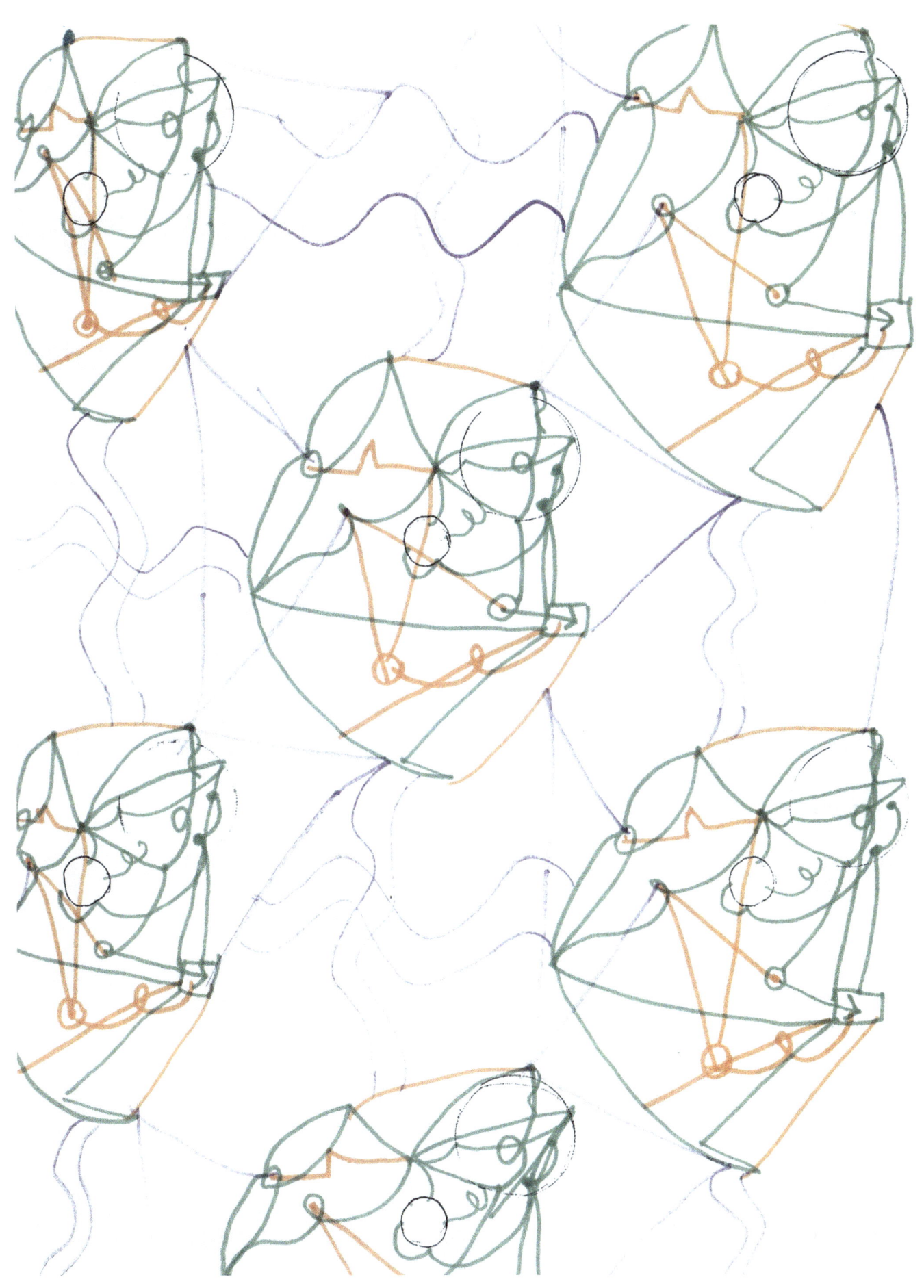

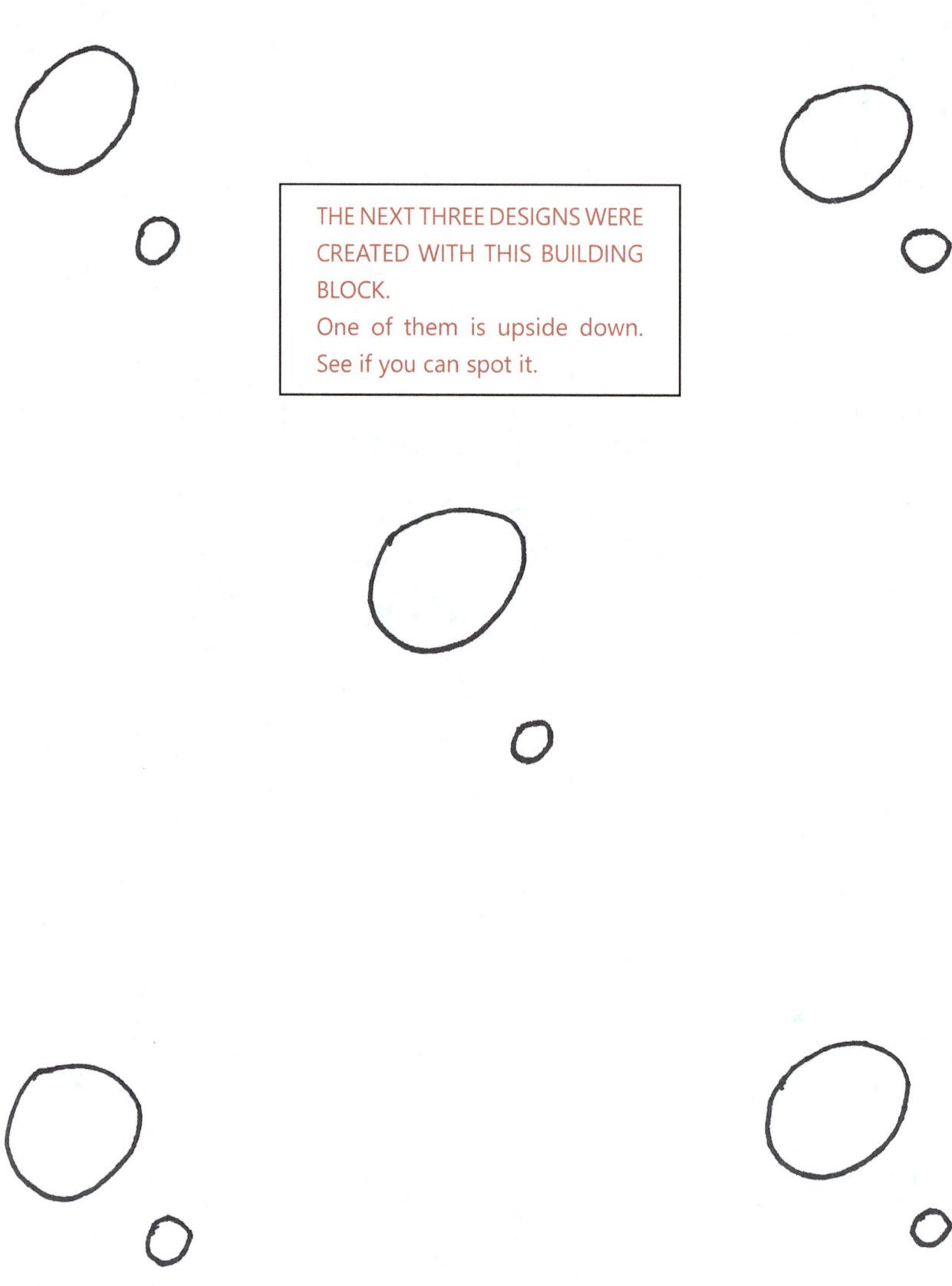

THE NEXT THREE DESIGNS WERE CREATED WITH THIS BUILDING BLOCK.
One of them is upside down.
See if you can spot it.

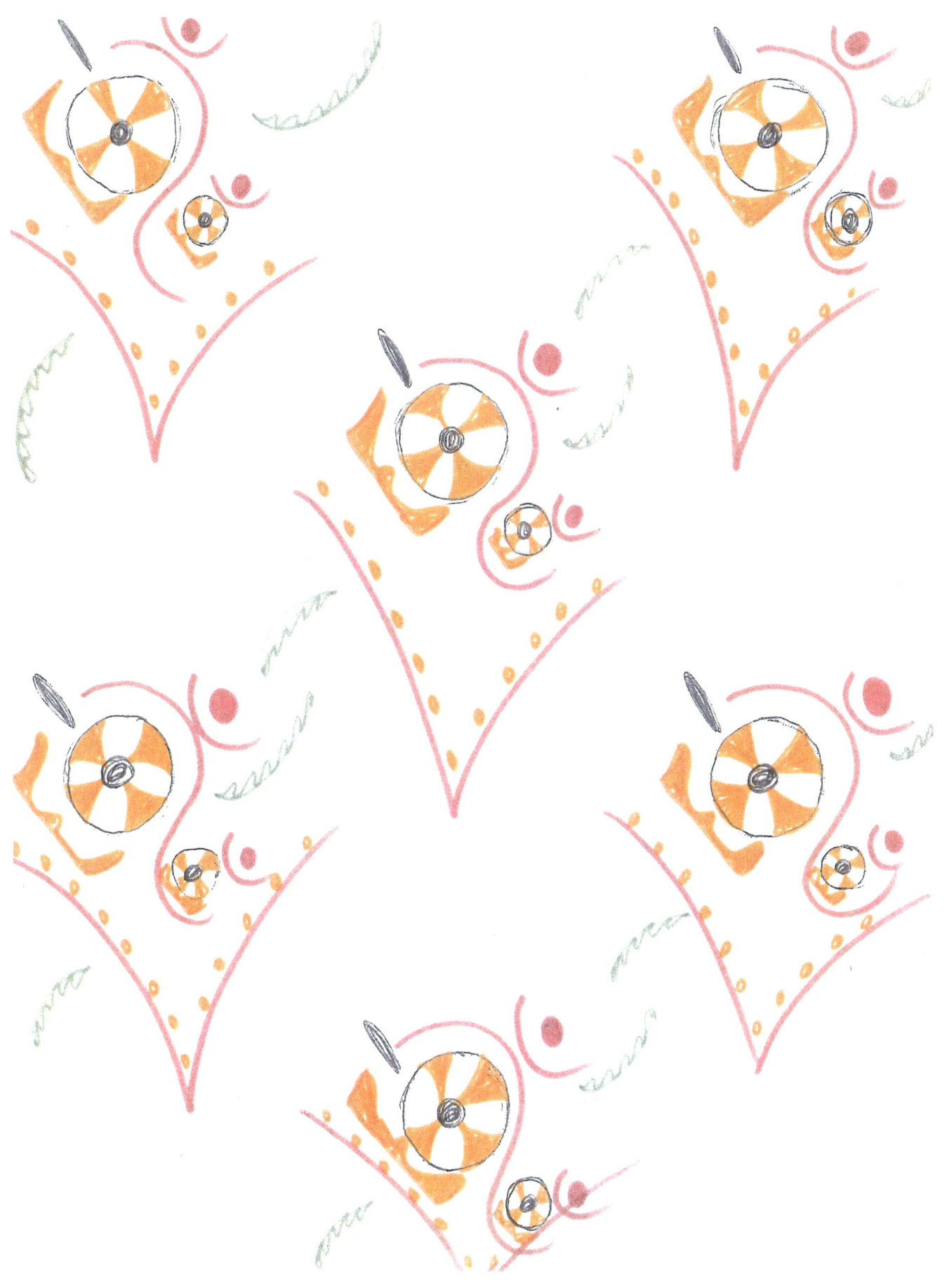

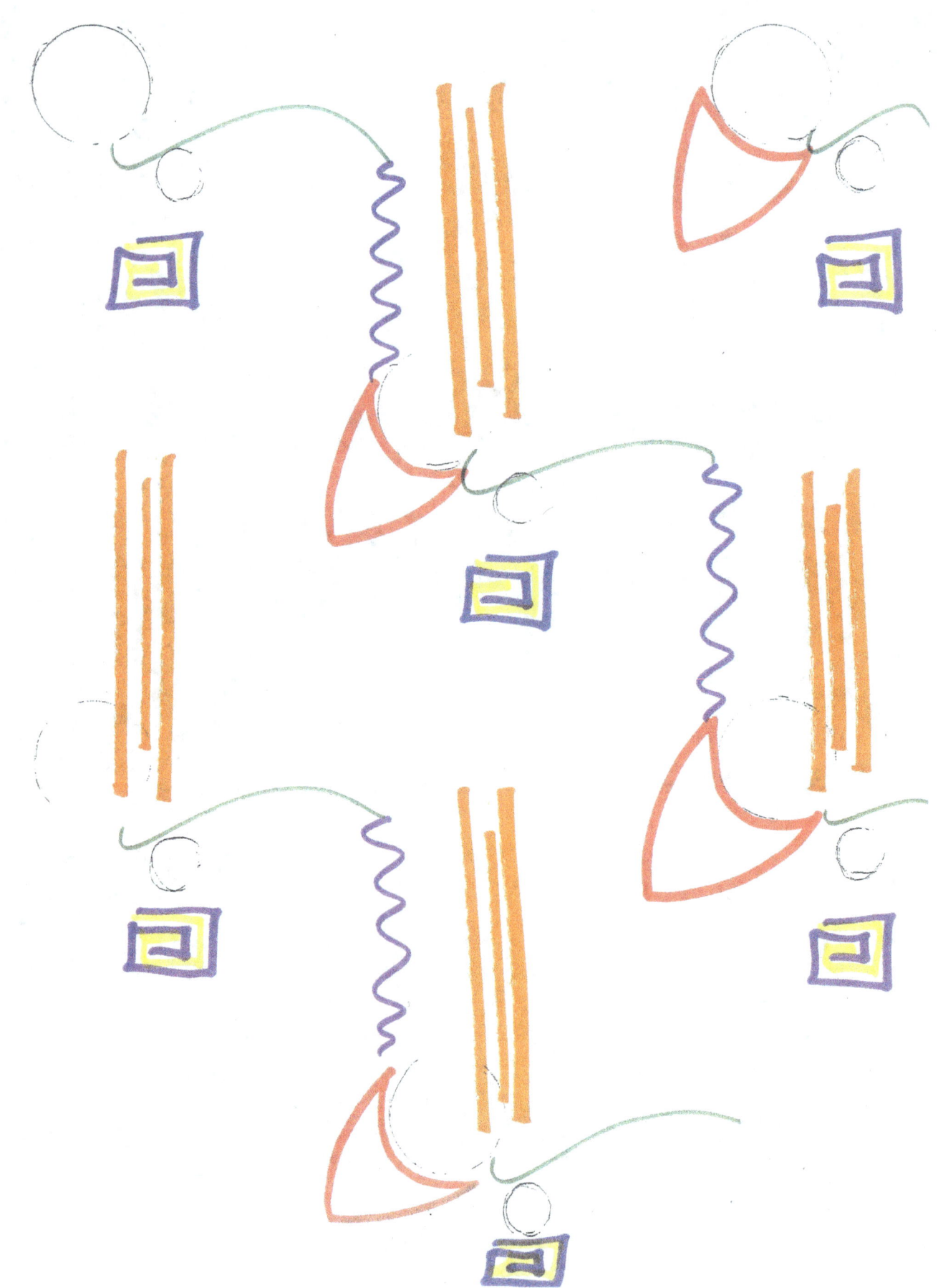

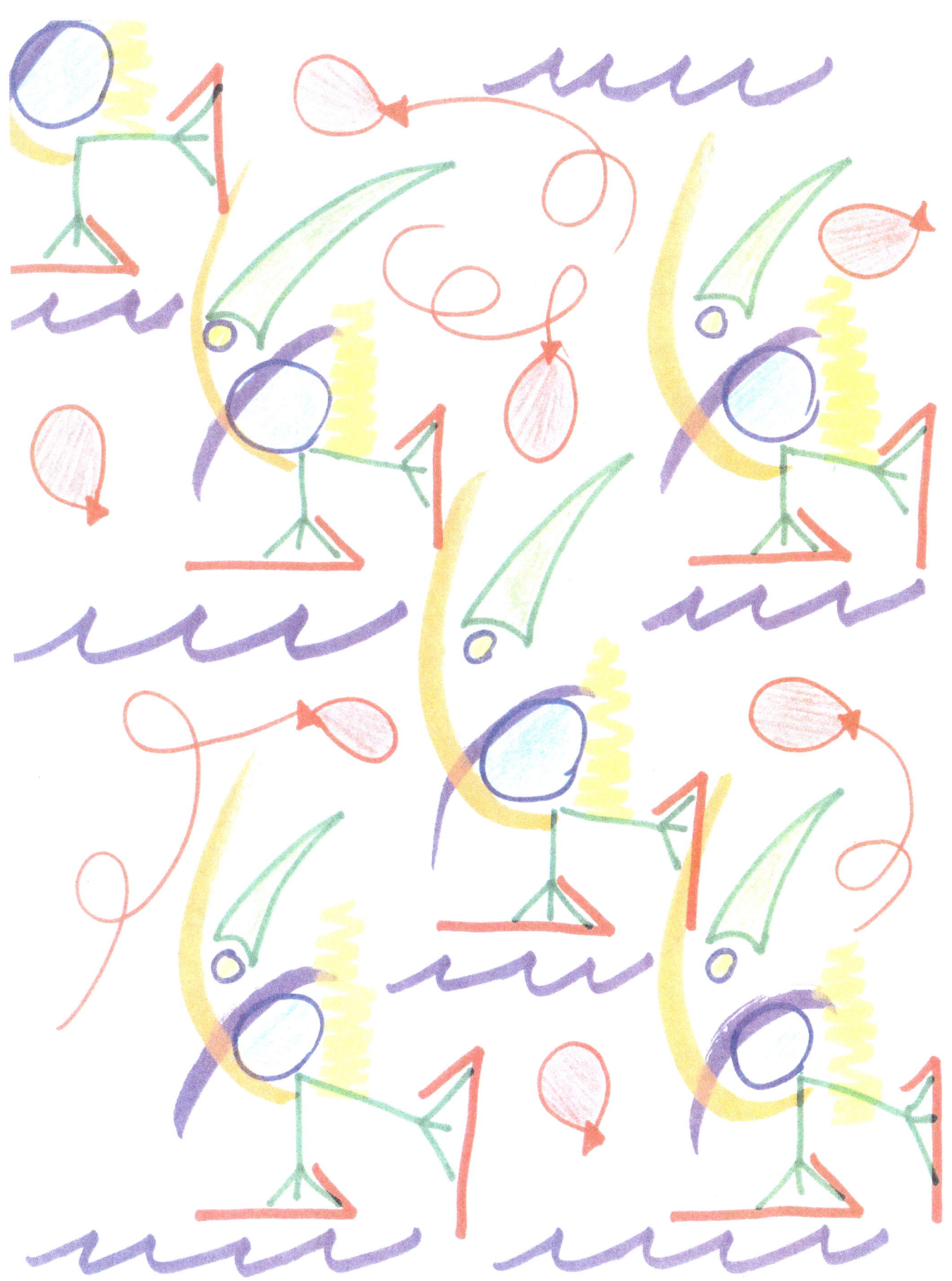

BUILDING BLOCK PAGES
FOR YOU TO USE

In the following pages are two copies each of six different building block sets, and a page of four reduced size building block sets, for you to use to create your own original designs. You can make additional copies to be sure you don't run out. You can also create building block pages of your own.

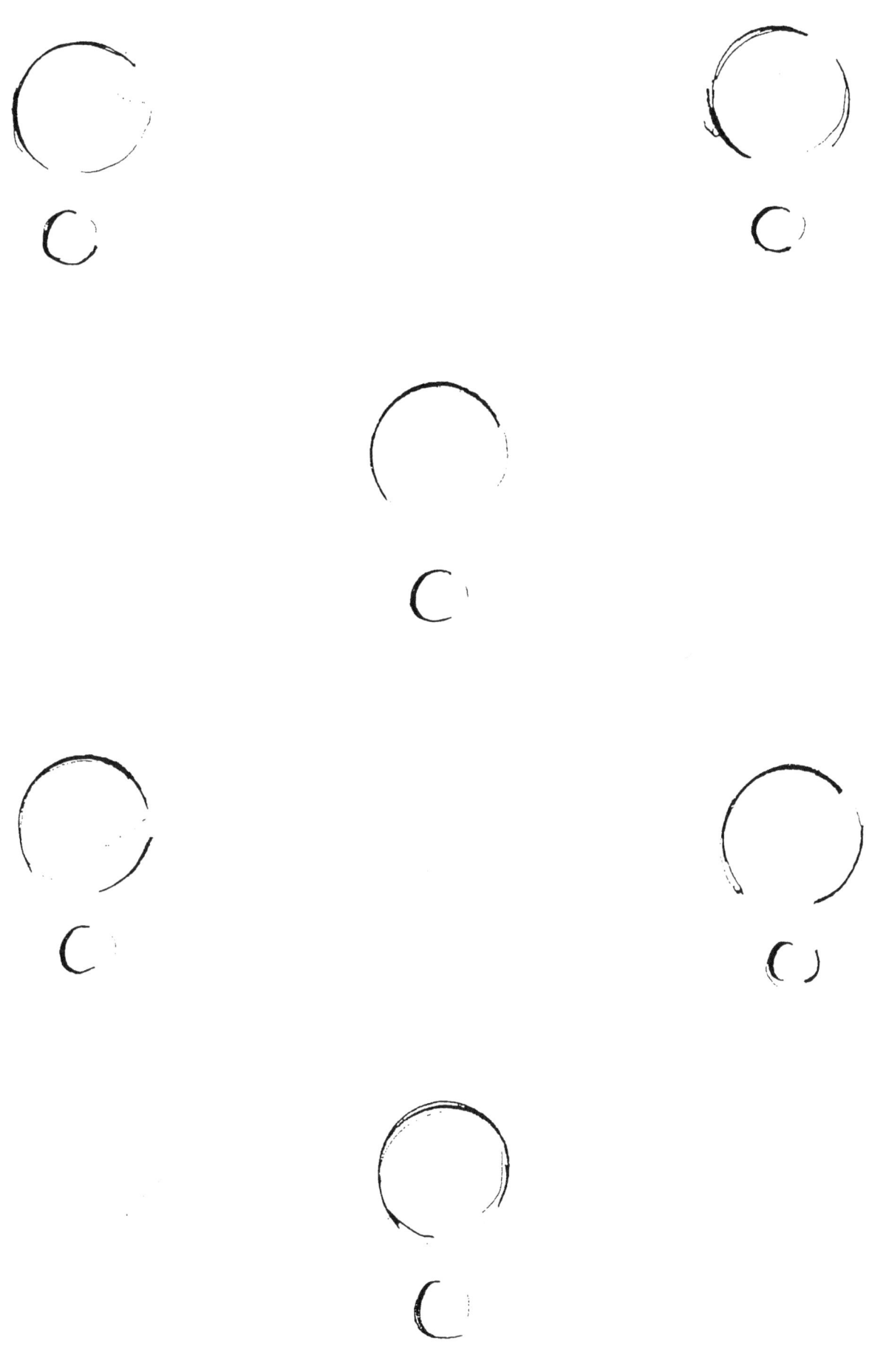

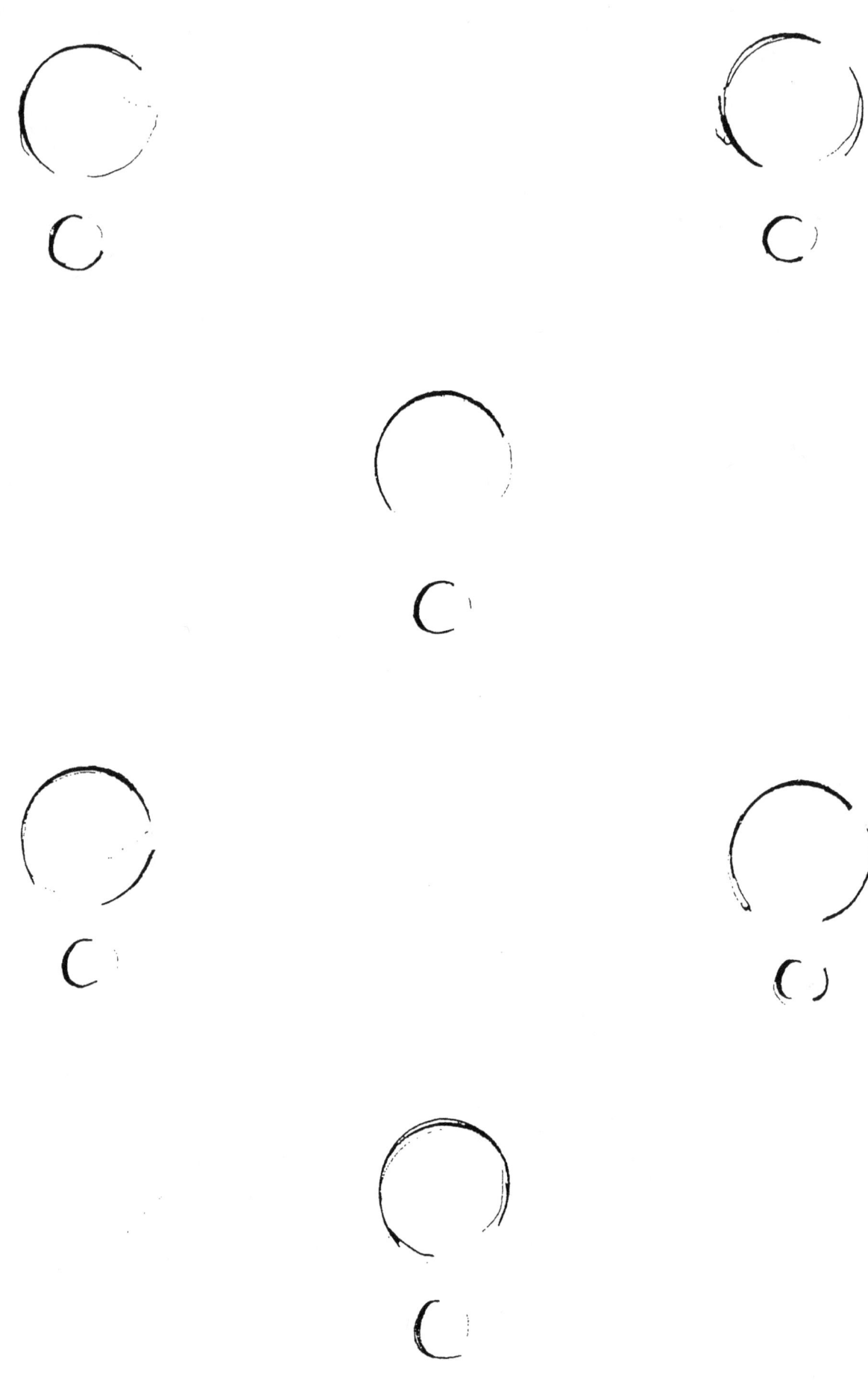

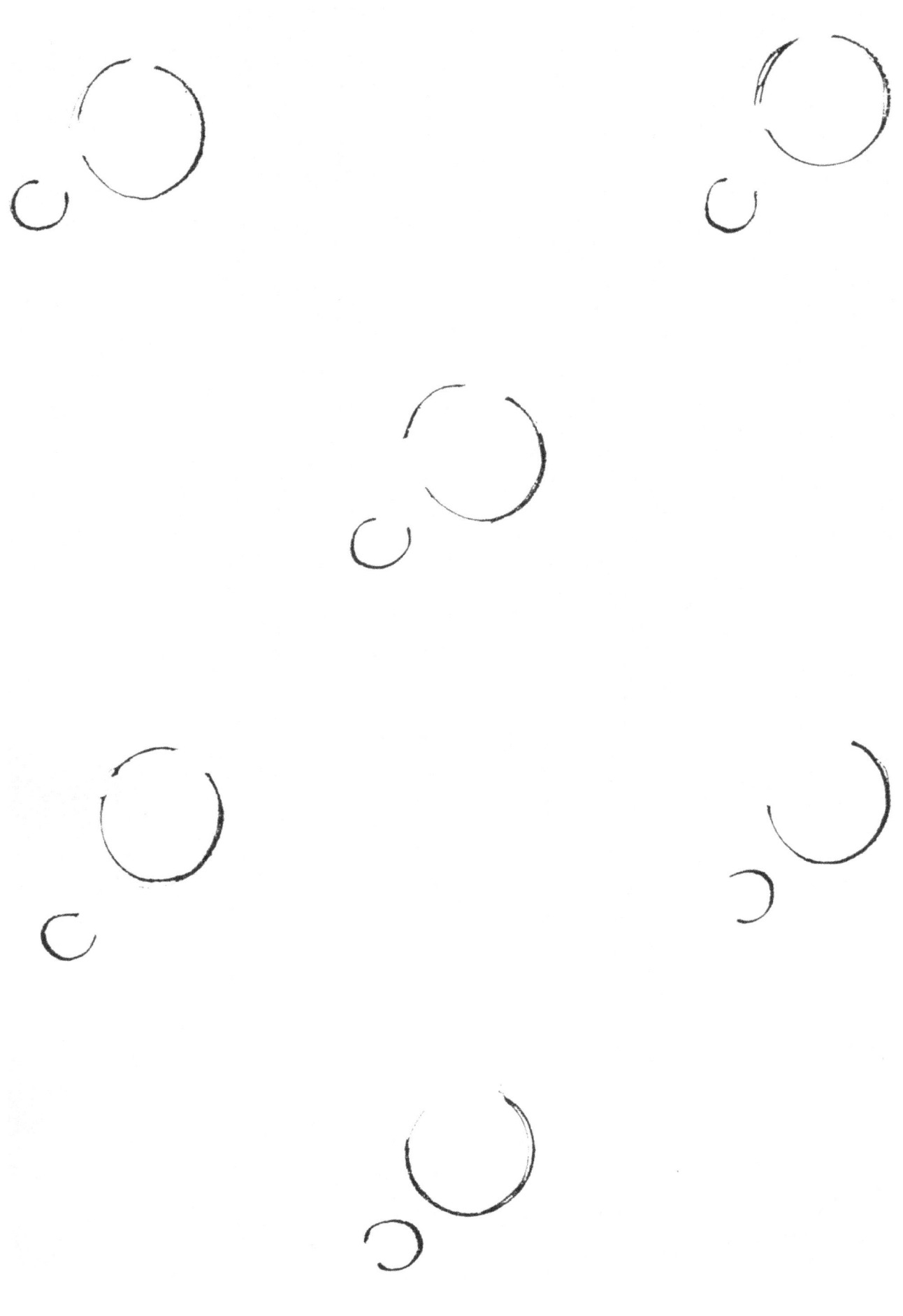

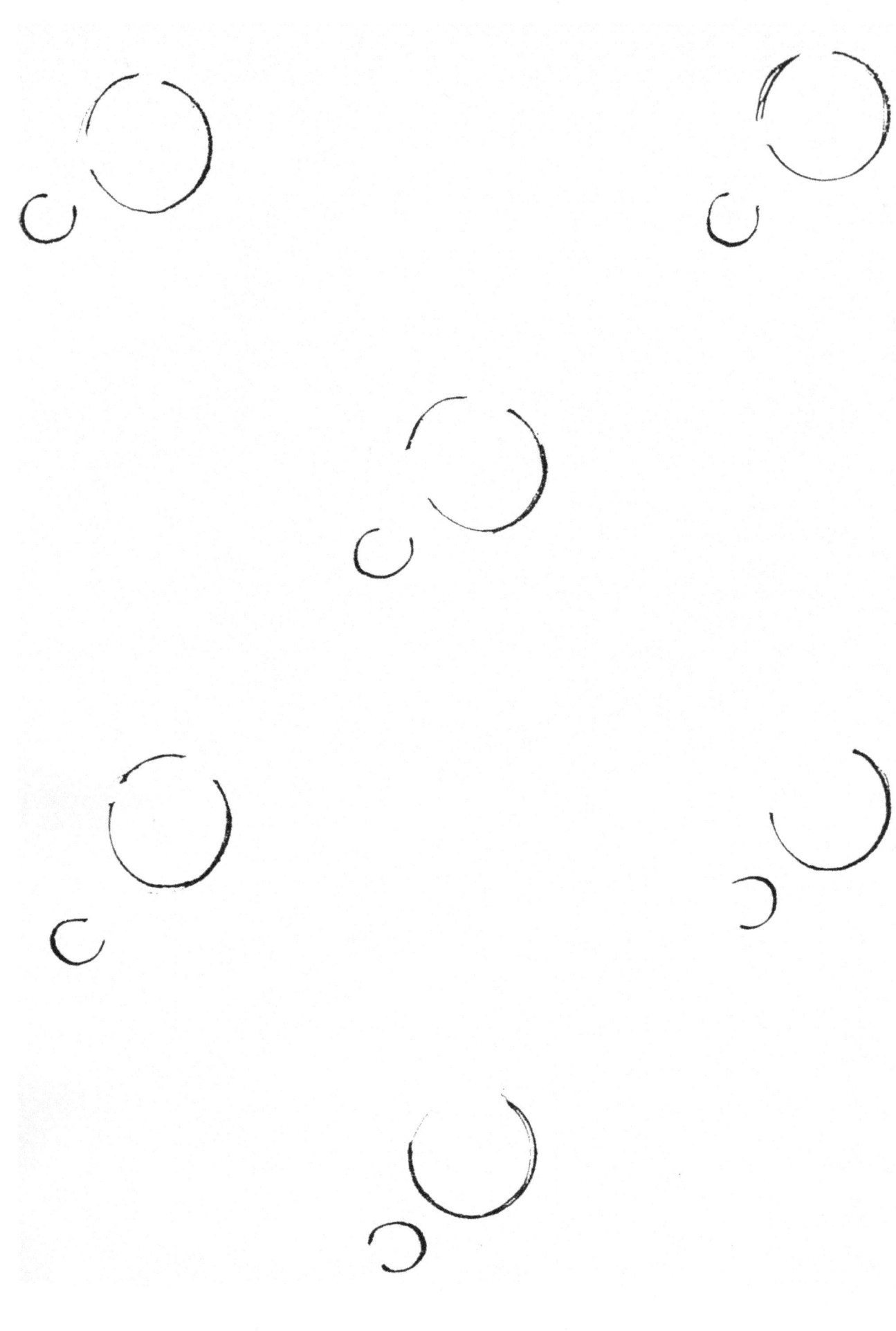

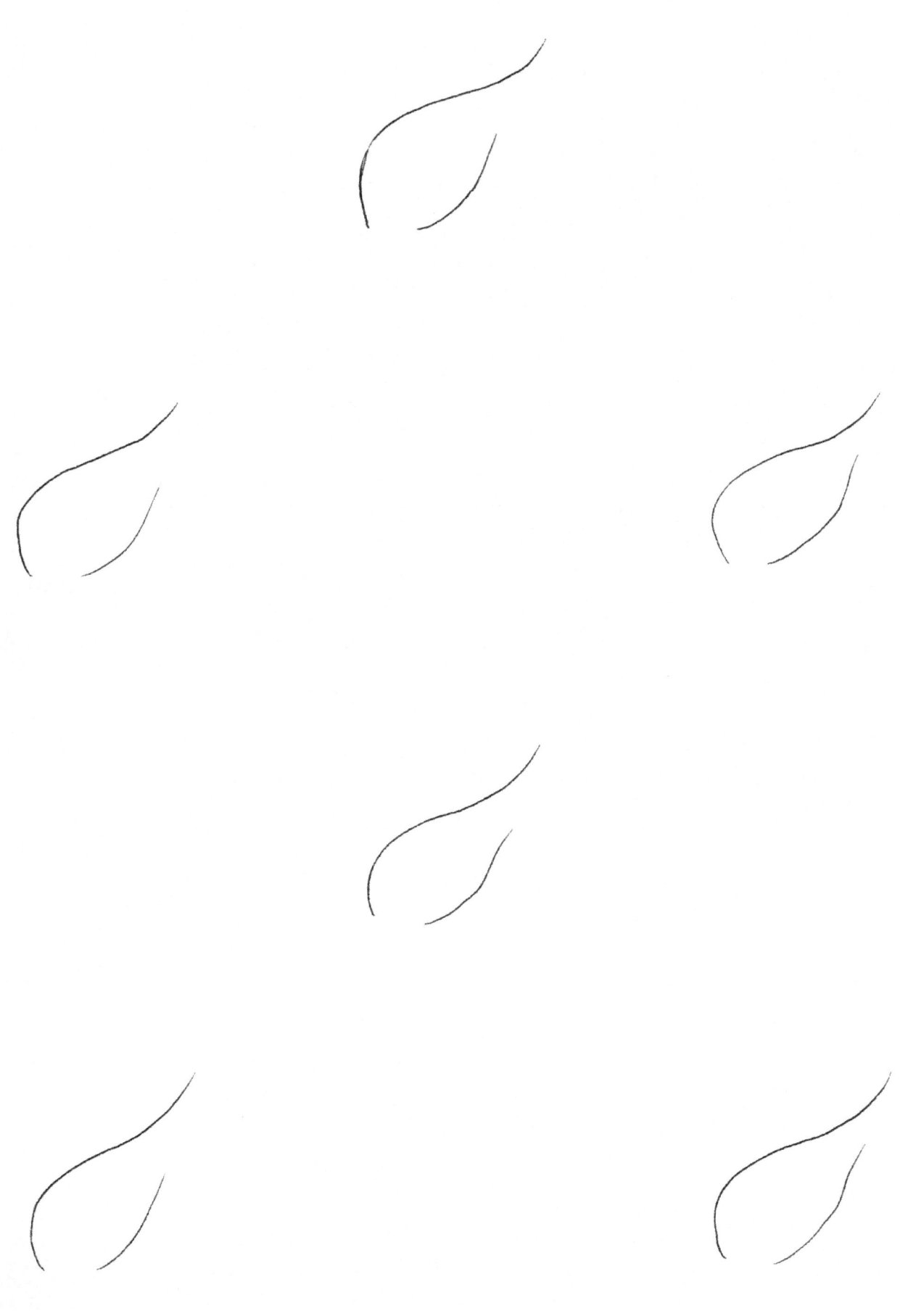

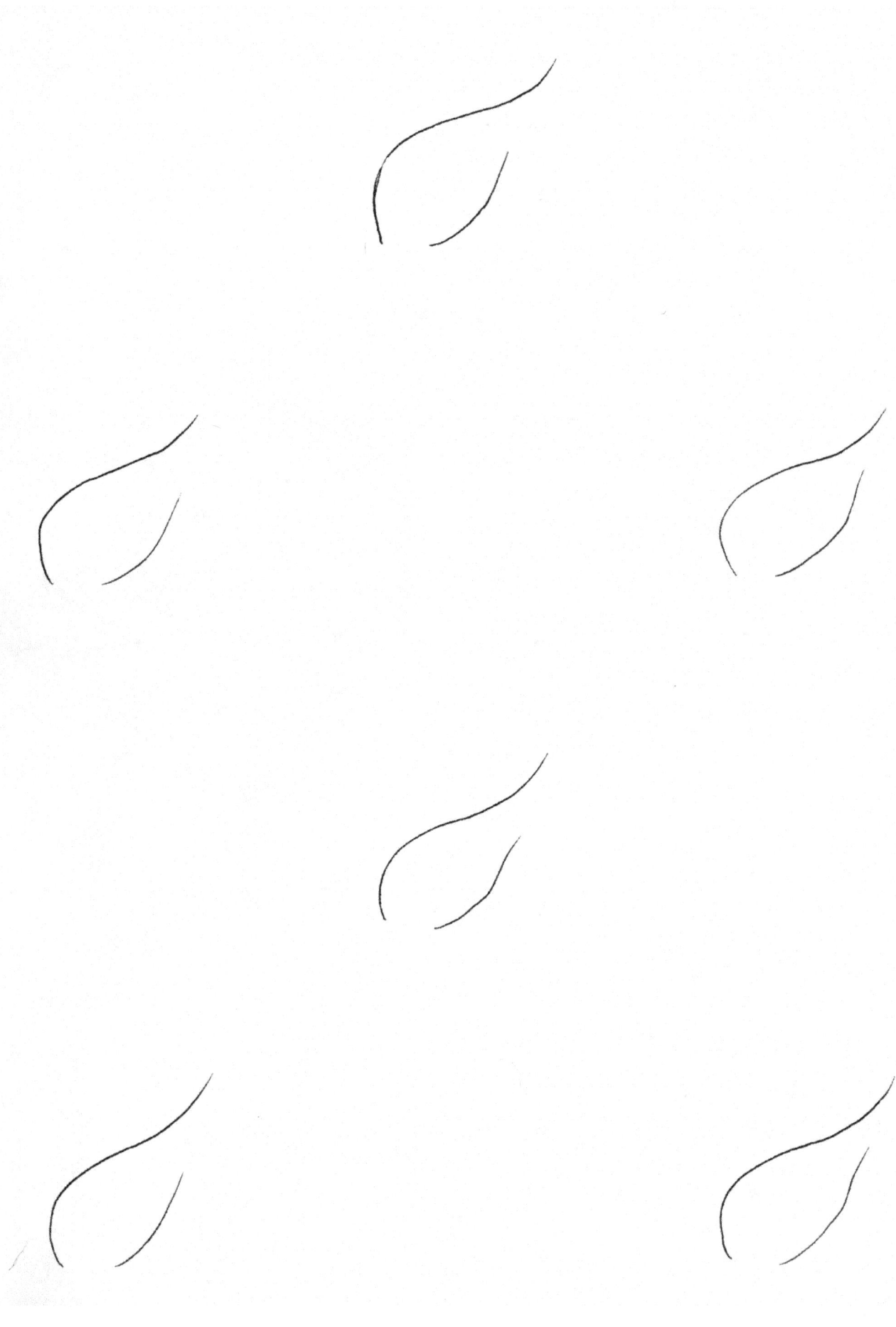

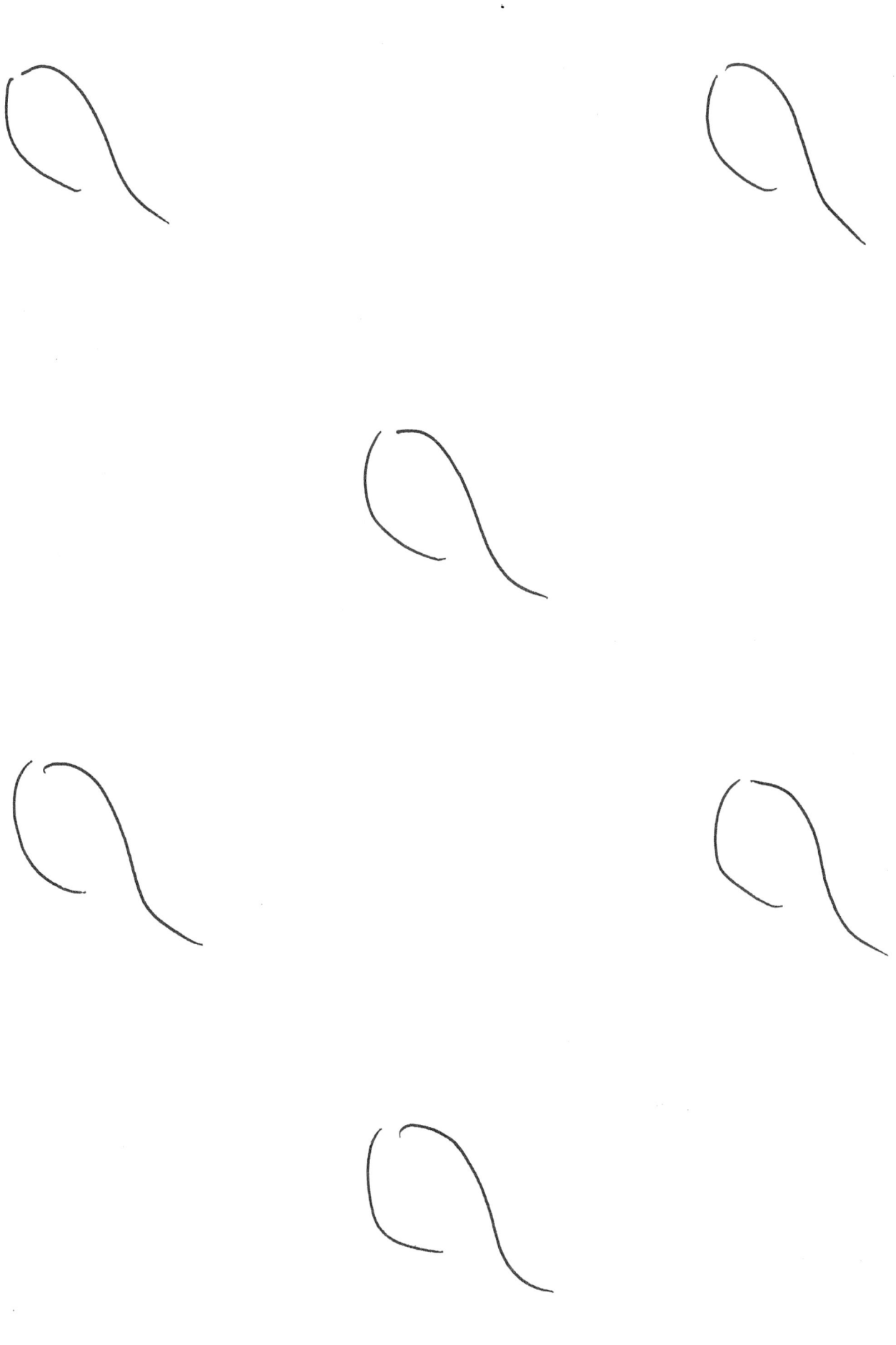

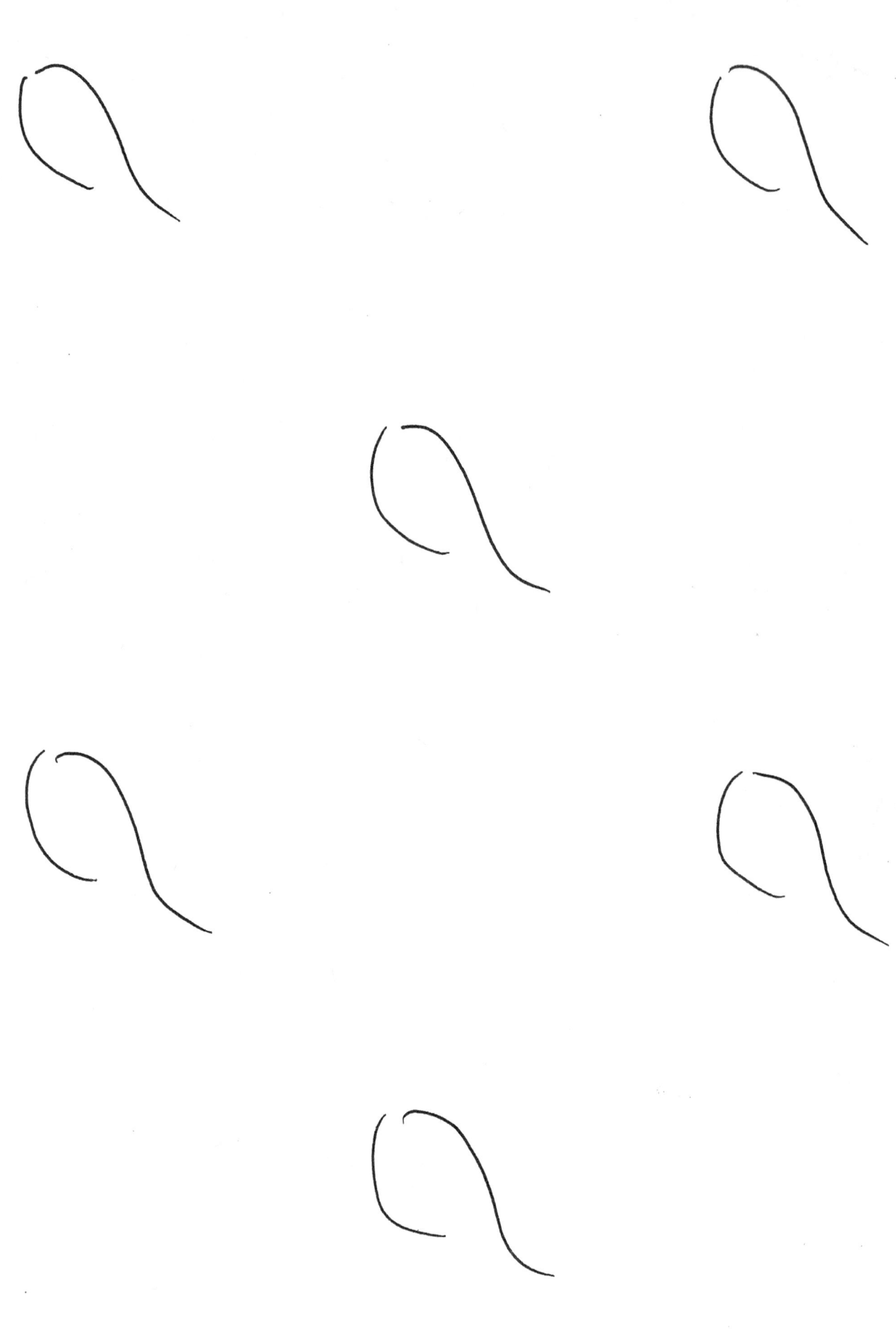

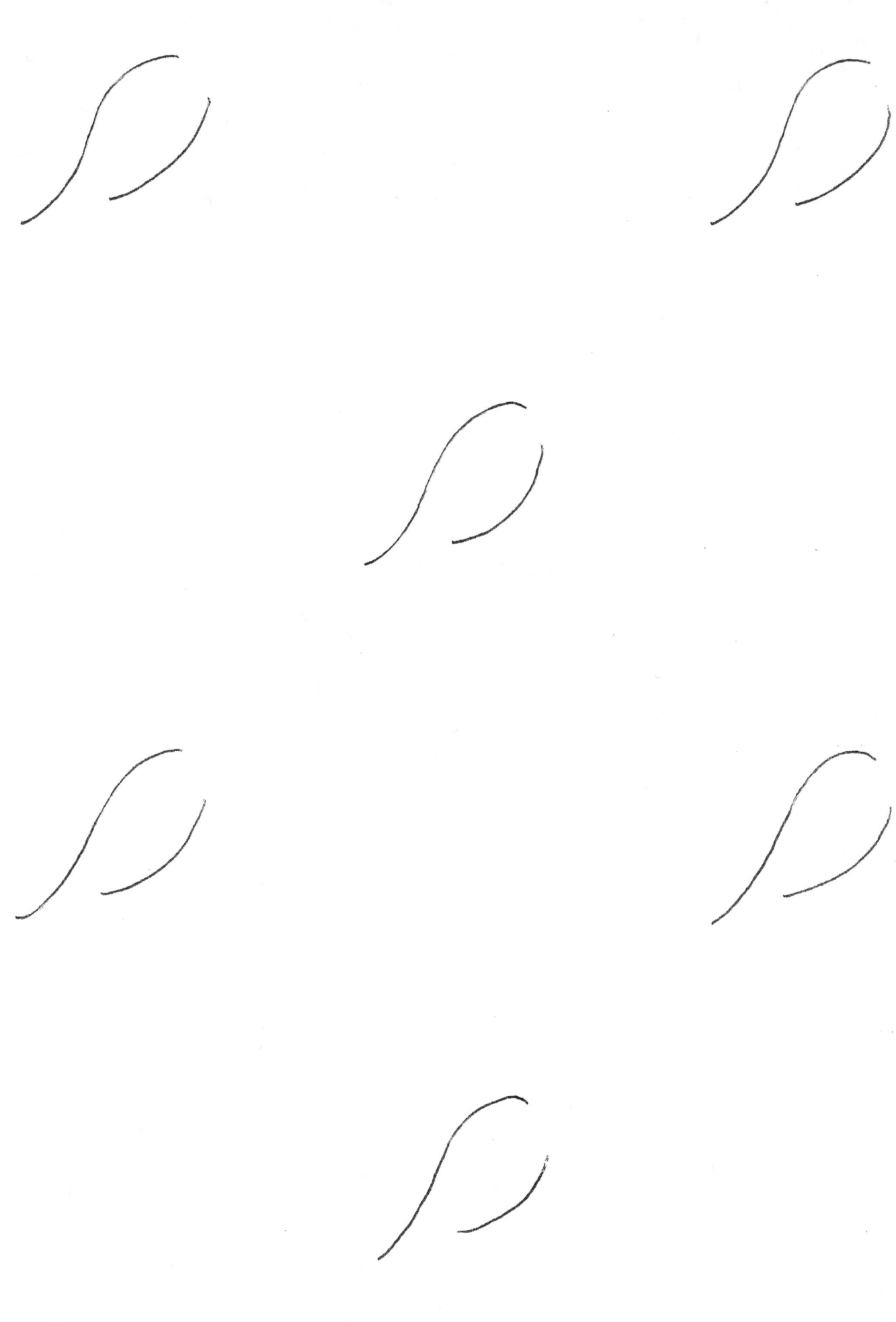

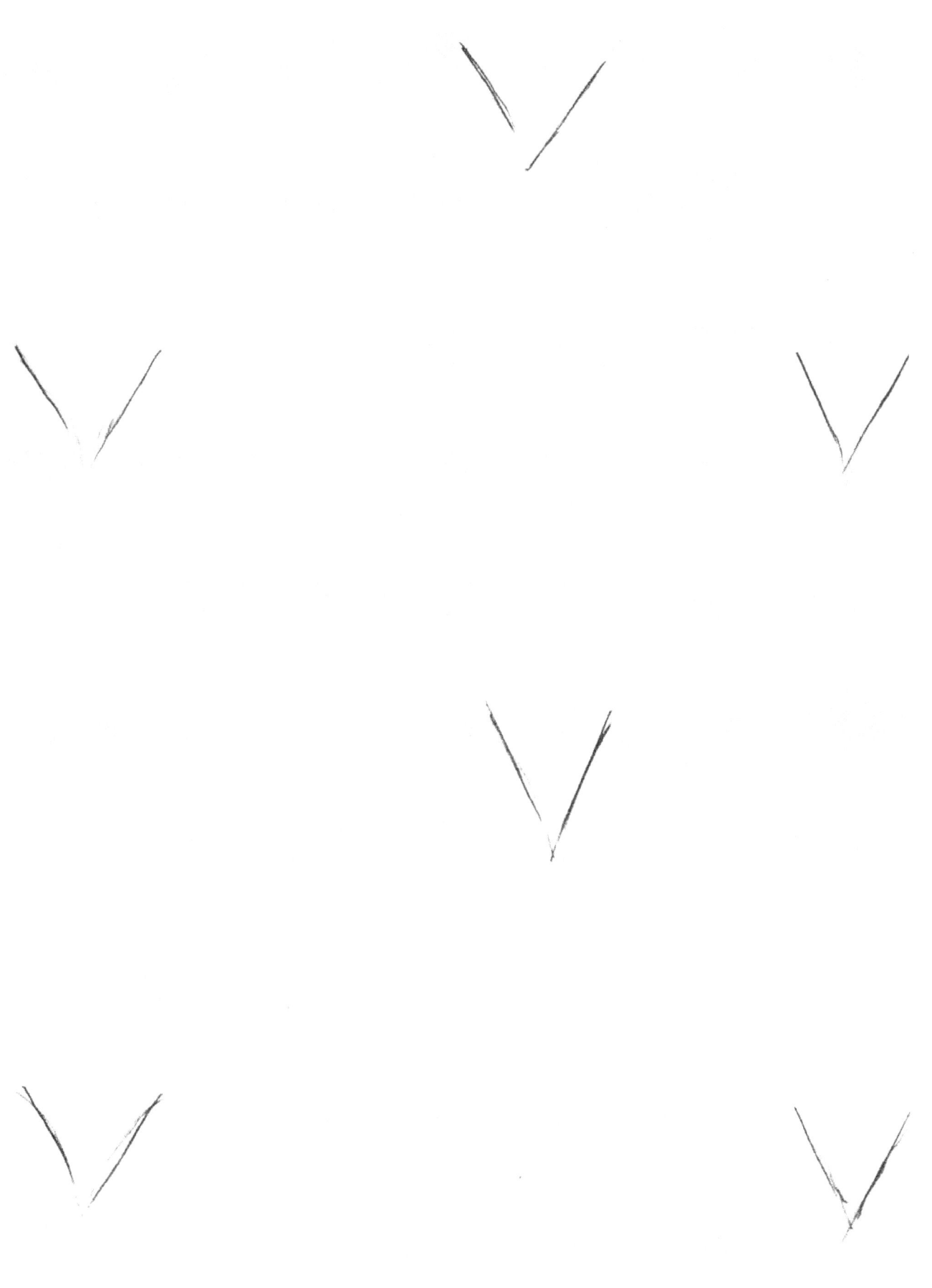

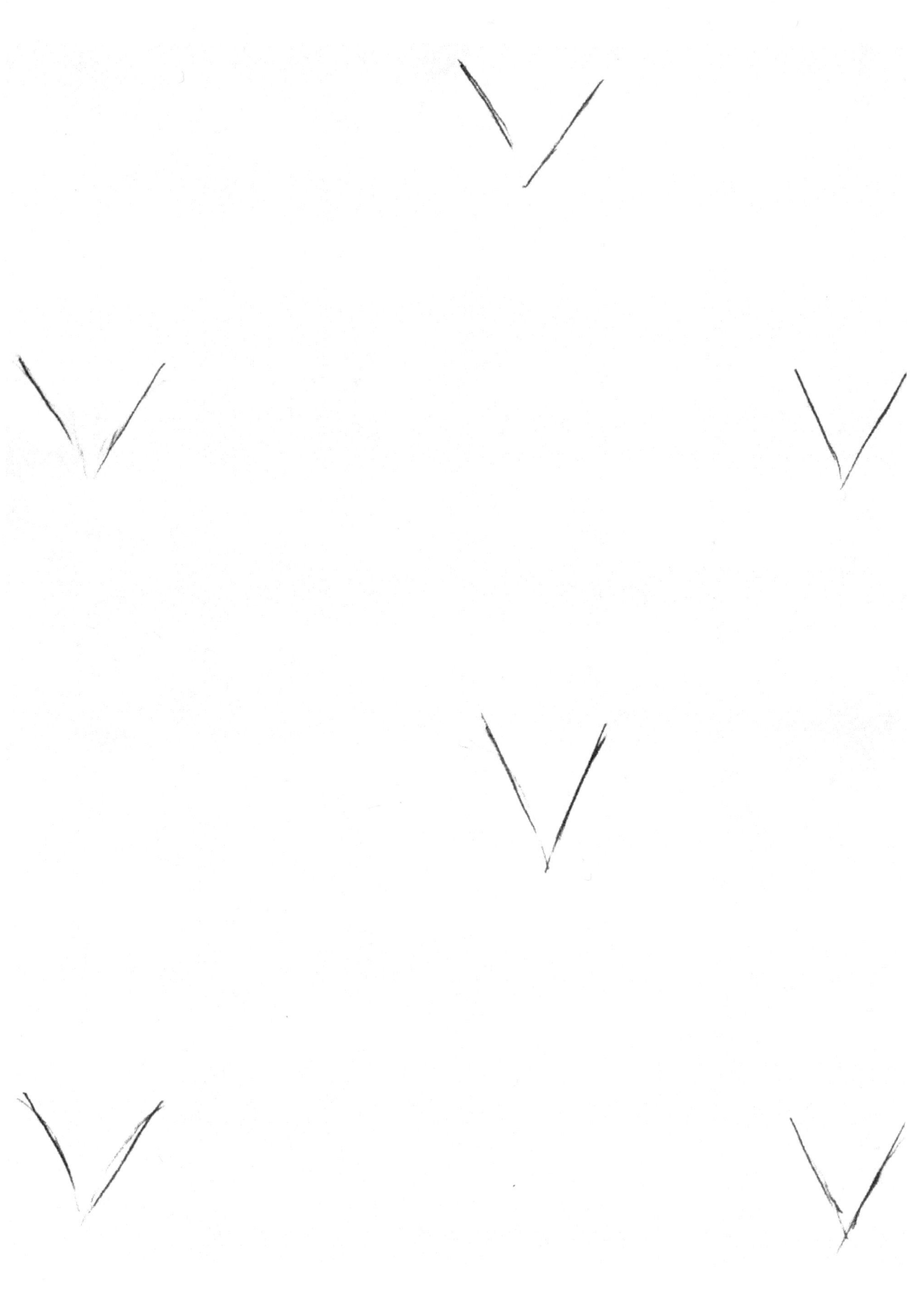

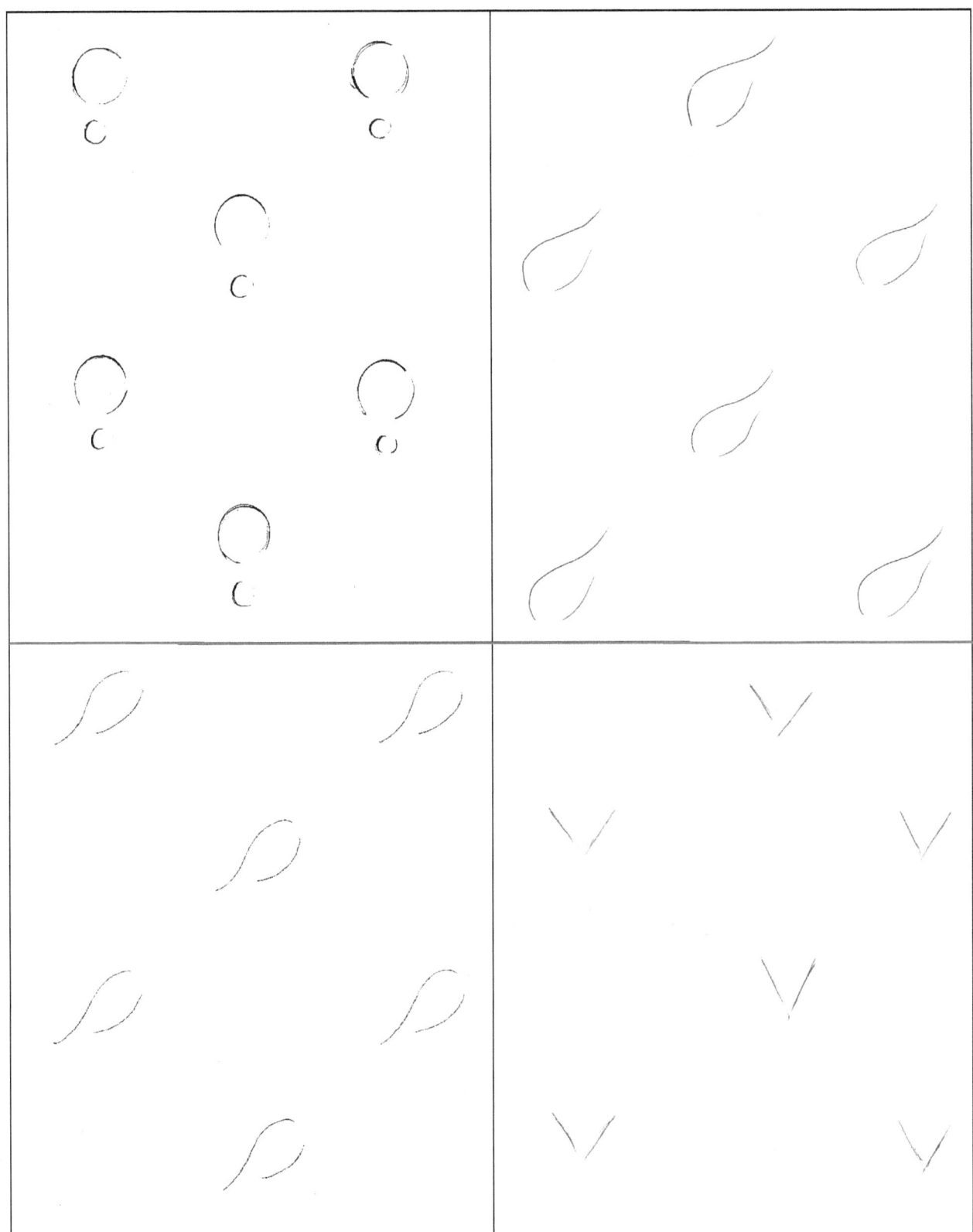

DESIGNS FROM CULTURES AROUND THE WORLD

Russian Ornament
of the Tadjik

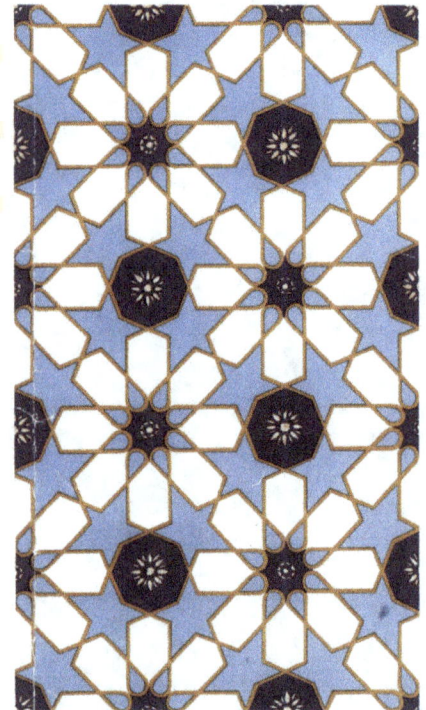

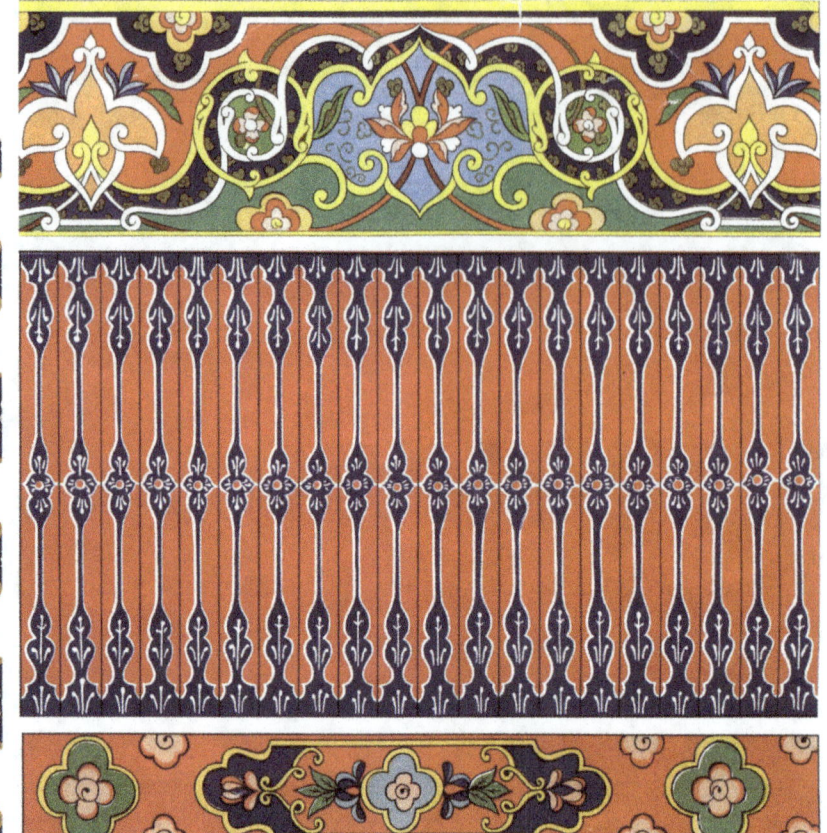

Victorian

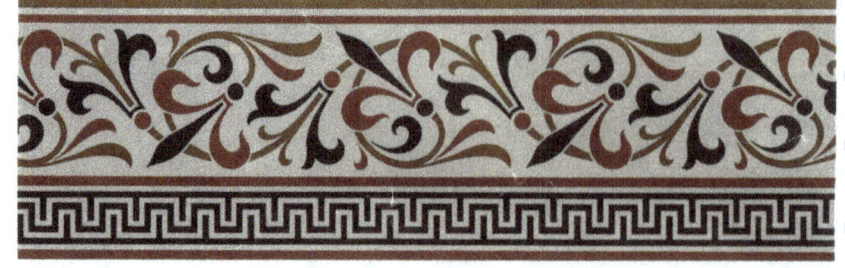

Celtic

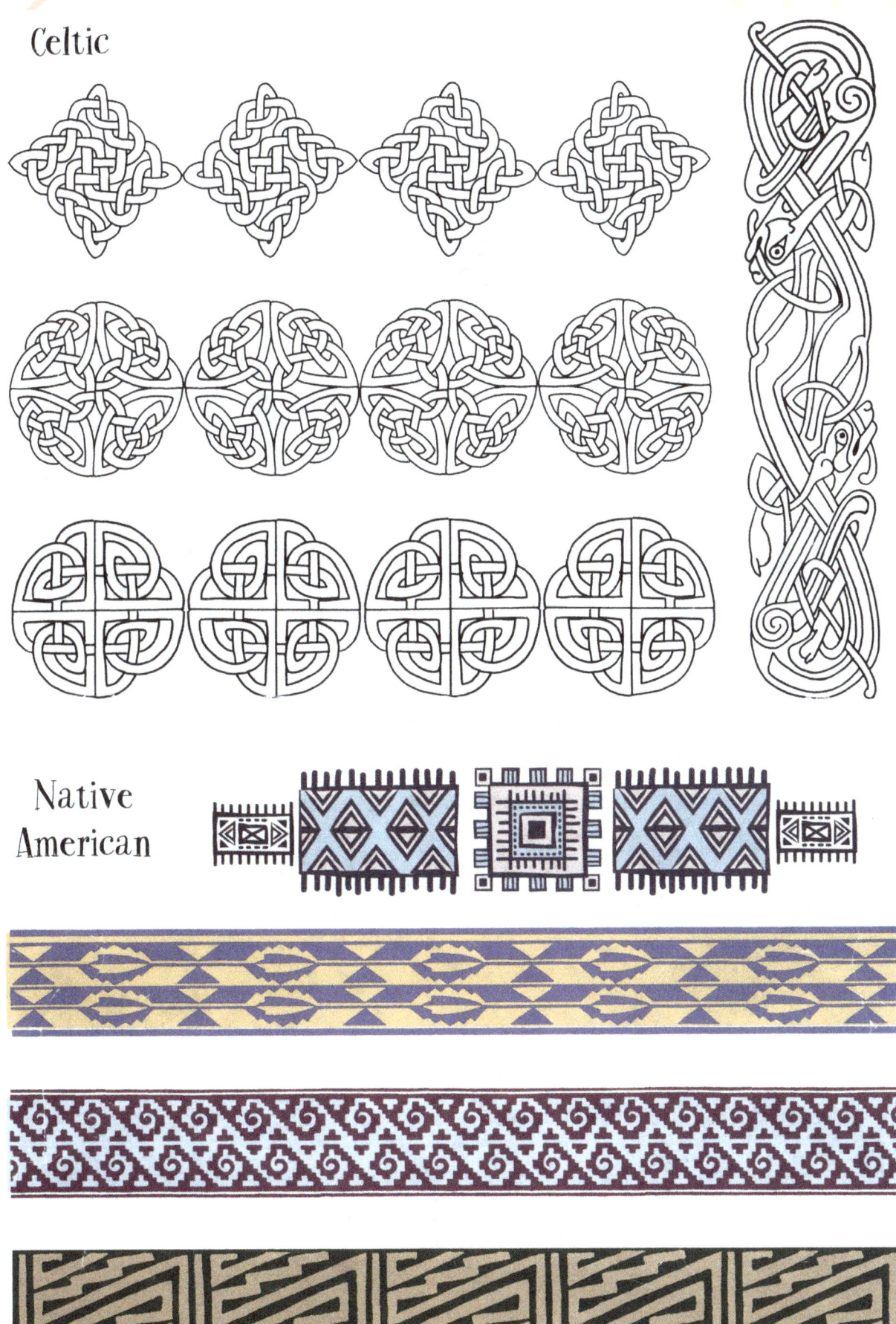

Native American

Roman
Mosaics

Roman
Borders

Ancient Egypt

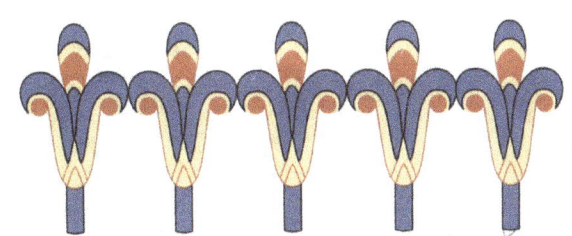

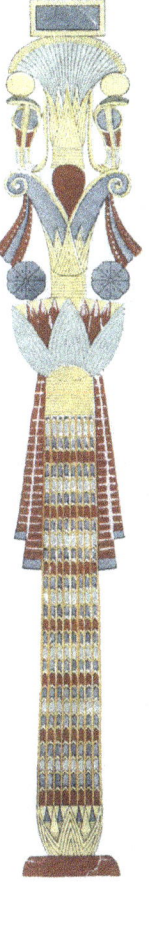

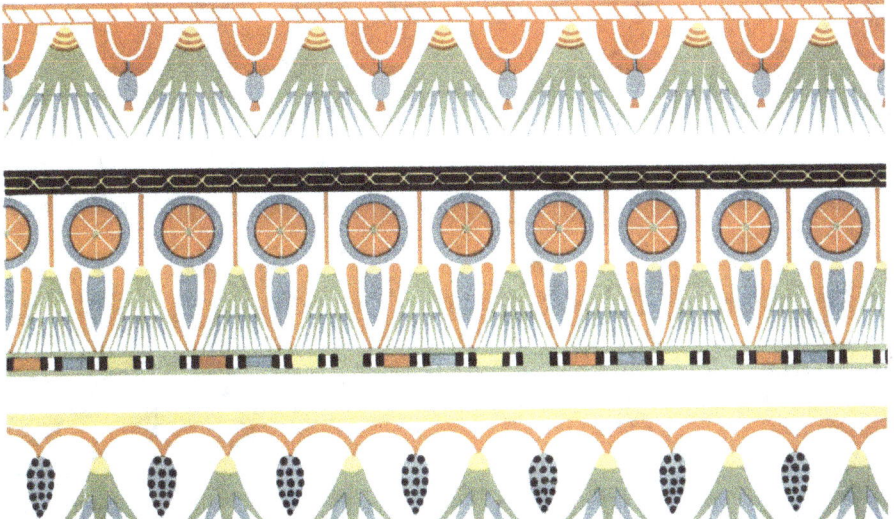

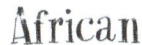

African

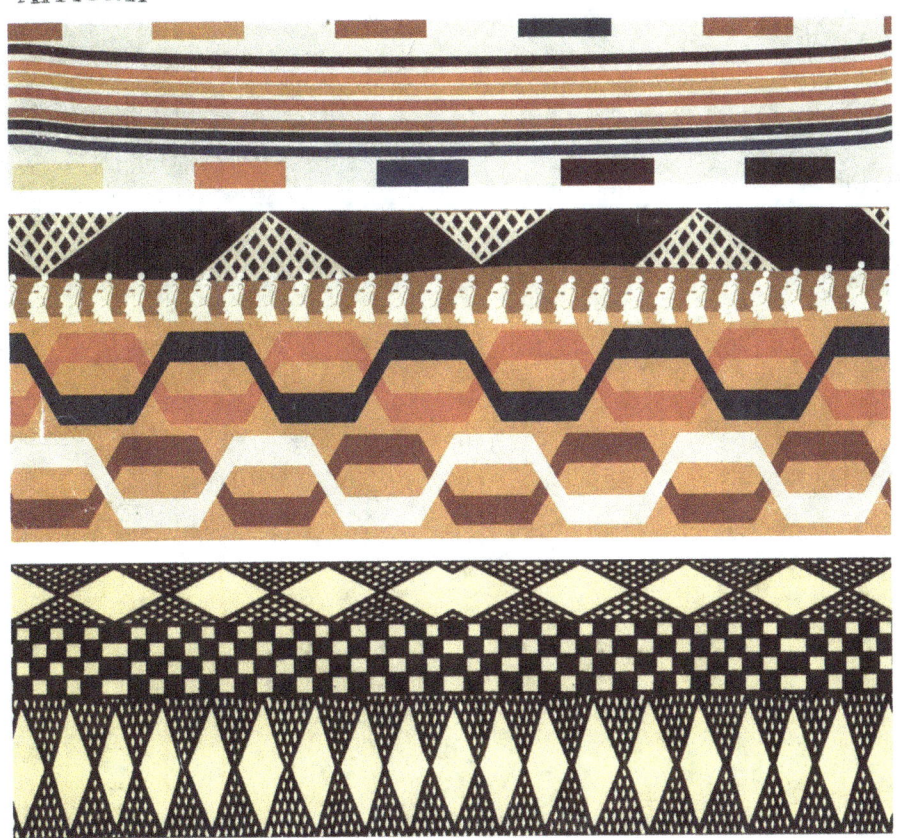

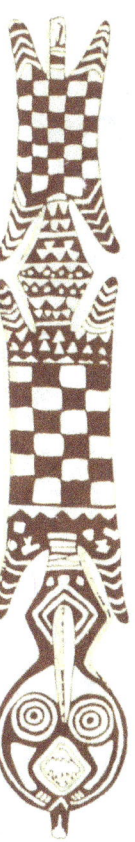

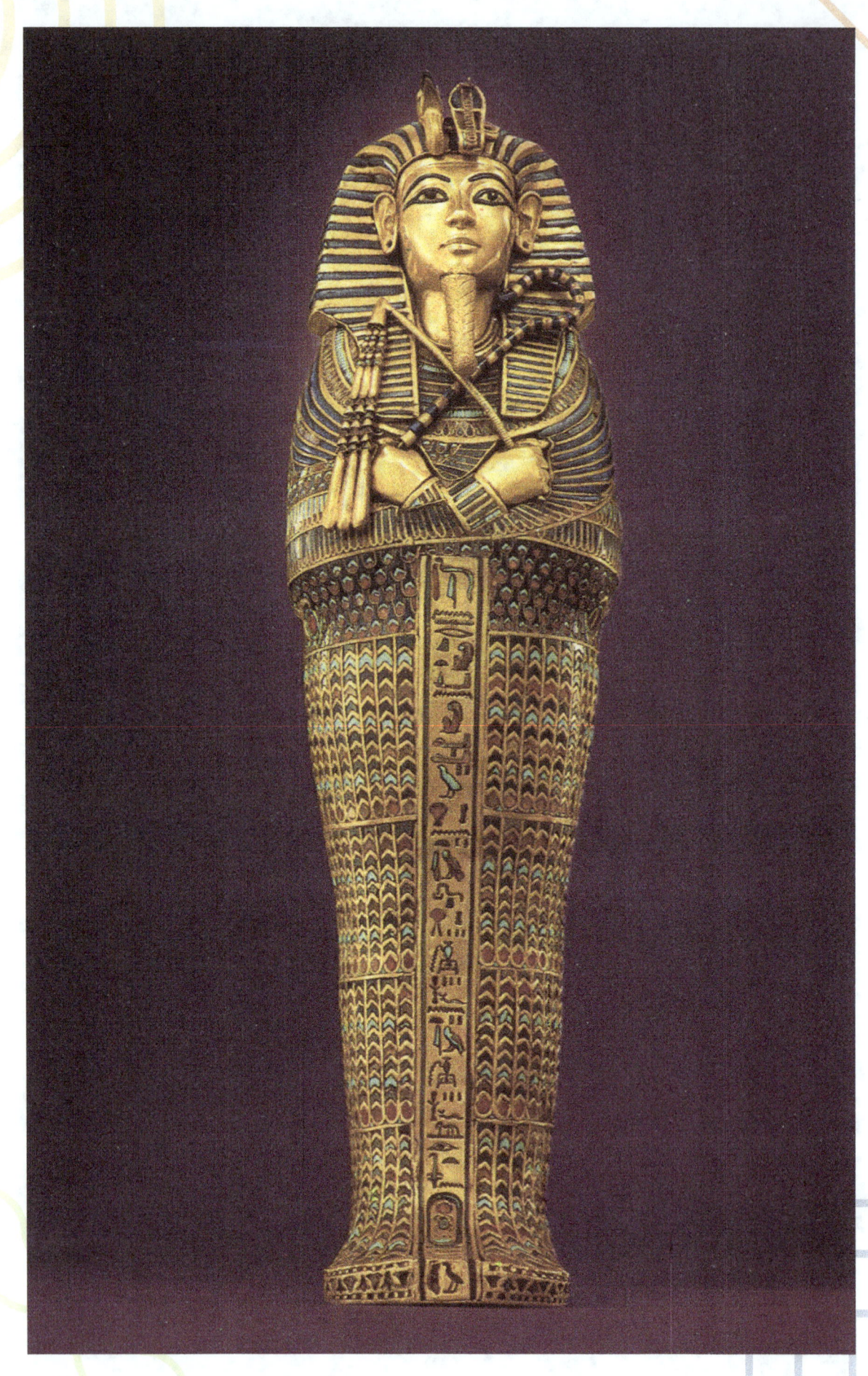

DEDICATION

I dedicate this book to my daughter, Katy Cobb (1953 – 1998). Writing this made me realize more than ever that she left a legacy of making this world a better place. Katy suffered a brain injury during birth, which caused mental and physical disabilities. She was never able to take care of her own daily needs, go to school, or live independently.

Despite her disabilities, Katy always had a special sparkle in her eyes. She had an amazing vocabulary and an incredible memory for people's names (even when she had not seen them in years) and for things she had heard in the past which she would repeat verbatim, often long afterwards and always in proper context. Katy integrated fully into the daily life of our family, our neighborhood and beyond, and she enriched us all. All who knew her agree that she brought positivity, happiness and joy to everyone she met. That made her transition to group homes easy for her when they became available later in her life.

As I was working on this book, I was reminded of an event that happened before Design and Sign was even an idea. Although Katy could not draw normally, she sure could scribble. One day, I left her with my eldest son and some scraps of paper while I ran errands. When I returned, he showed me how he had added to her scribbles and created rocket ships and other pictures and designs. Katy's scribbling had become an art activity!

Katy loved music of all kinds. She was never far from a portable radio or a record player. When hospitalized with terminal cancer, her music made her feel better; she was listening to Carole King's *Tapestry*, her all-time favorite album, when she died at the age of 45. In her memory, my family established the Katy Cobb Music Therapy Program at Union Hospital in Terre Haute, Indiana. After many years, there is now a full-time music therapist on staff at the hospital.

ACKNOWLEDGEMENTS

So many people have helped me bring Design and Sign to life that there is not nearly enough space to name them all. It surely would never have happened without my friend Melanie Zeck, whose enthusiasm, ideas, research, and persistent cheerleading finally got me across the finish line. I also owe much to my extended family of nieces, nephews and their children, who for decades "field tested" the idea of design and sign; most of the examples of completed designs in the book are theirs. Mary Jo Rajala and Kelly Rajala, especially, gave me persistent and much needed encouragement over the years to start and pursue this project. My great nieces Amy Kreft Green and Allison Kreft Abad were so generous with their time and skills developing the book's cover; the final selection is Amy's design. My sons Bill and Peter Cobb did a lot of the hands-on work that turned my stacks of raw materials into the book you now hold in your hands. And, of course, Katy's wonderful spirit has been with me and provided inspiration through it all.